ENHANCED PEOPLE SKILLS

The pathway to success in all areas of your life

Never settle For less than Extraordinary.

John Terhune

ISBN: 1503180999
ISBN 13: 9781503180994

DEDICATION

I dedicate this book to the memory of my father, Colonel Burke C. Terhune. I watched my father use his amazing people skills throughout his distinguished twenty-one-year career in the US Air Force, followed by a very successful civilian career. Whether you were a highly successful business person or a waiter at a restaurant, Burke had the ability to become your friend within one conversation. In my life I have rarely seen anyone more universally liked and respected. He knew how to treat people and valued people not for what they were, but for who they were as fellow human beings. I owe a great deal of my people skill set to the example that he set in my life simply by living his life with integrity and joy. Thanks, Colonel.

ACKNOWLEDGMENTS

A sincere thanks to several people who made this book possible. As always I thank and appreciate my beautiful and wonderful wife, Pat. Our thirty years of marriage have been a joy. Beyond being the heart-throb of my life, she always has been and is today my dearest friend. She also happens to be a great proofreader and editor and worked her magic again with this book. Her opinion is something that I value so much and when she told me she loved the book, I knew it was a book that would make a difference for people.

I also want to thank my great friend and colleague, Jack Lannom, for writing the foreword to this book. Jack is an amazingly talented author, consultant, and speaker. People First, the program he pioneered, is by far the best cultural transformation and leadership development program that I have ever seen. If your company has not yet become a People First Certified Company, it simply isn't working and performing up to its full potential. I am honored to call Jack my friend and colleague.

Finally, I want to thank my highly valued consultant and friend, Yolanda Harris. In short, Yolanda makes me look good. She is a remarkably smart business coach with a huge heart for helping people win. Her company, the Keynote Group, represents some of the world's top authors and keynote speakers. I am very honored that she took me on as a client.

CONTENTS

CONTENTS

FOREWORD

One of the greatest honors of my life was when John Terhune asked me if I would write the foreword to his new book, *Enhanced People Skills*. Let me tell you why I was so excited about doing this for my good friend whom I have known for over twenty years.

Of all the people I have met in my forty-plus years on this planet as a leadership consultant, John Terhune is the most qualified person I know to write the most powerful and practical book on enhanced people skills. I can assure you that he embodies everything he teaches in this masterpiece—John Terhune is a walking billboard of how to treat people with dignity, respect, and honor.

In other words, John lives what he preaches. When he told me that he was writing a book on enhanced people skills the first thing that came to my mind was, "If John Terhune is going to take the time to write all that he has learned and practiced on this subject, I can't wait to get a copy of his book and devour it." I know that it will be a great read. And it lived up to and exceeded everything that I have come to expect from this extremely accomplished leader and personal friend.

Enhanced People Skills is the finest book that I have ever read on the art and science of personal development. This is not written from an ivory-tower perspective devoid of practical application; John supplies his readers with real-world strategies that a person could read and immediately use to improve upon their people skills that same day.

As I was reading *Enhanced People Skills*, I was so impressed with the fact that John covered all of the areas a person must master to go beyond good and become great with their people skills. Moreover, his writing style is very refreshing in that it is not only highly instructional, but very inspirational as well. A John Terhune book is not boring—you will find yourself glued to every page soaking in the wisdom of each new enhanced people skill, realizing that this is the book you have been looking for all of your life.

I am making *Enhanced People Skills* required reading for all of my clients. If you have children in high school or college this is the book for them—it will give them one of the greatest competitive advantages in their personal and professional lives.

The bottom line in being successful in life and business is creating great relationships and great results. Now, turn the page and learn how to apply enhanced people skills to reap a harvest of improved relationships and results.

Jack Lannom
CEO, People First International

INTRODUCTION

I've had this book forming in my head over the last thirty years. As I have had an opportunity to observe human behavior and interaction from various perspectives, I am more convinced today than ever before that great people skills are the key to success in all areas of one's life. The great news about this thesis is that anyone, with a diligent effort, can develop his or her people skills to the point where a person will begin to see marked improvement in business and personal relationships, thus enhancing success and happiness.

I want to take a moment to give you some insight on my background so that you have a clear picture of my perspectives before you begin on your journey to enhanced people skills. By education, I am an attorney. I spent ten years of my life as a trial lawyer. I was the chief felony prosecutor in a northern Florida jurisdiction. If you are at all familiar with trial work you should know that regardless of the facts of the case, it all comes down to whom you select to sit as jurors. I first began to recognize this fact when I invested a year of my life watching every jury selection in Leon County, where Florida State University Law School was located. I was very fortunate to attend a great law school that was located one block away from the First District Court of Appeals, two blocks away from the Florida Supreme Court, three blocks away from the state legislature, and four blocks away from the county courthouse where cases were being tried every week. With the dream of becoming a trial lawyer, I spent a great deal of time during my second of three years of law school either watching jury selections or attending acting classes at the theater department at FSU. The end goal of observing jury selections and taking acting classes was to become an expert in trends in jury selections and outcomes and to become a person who could command the courtroom by enhancing my speaking and presence skills.

During my year of watching every jury selection, I began to recognize a subtle but very important dynamic taking place. The trial lawyers had an additional hurdle to leap if they were going to win their case—it wasn't just about putting the right people in the seats; they also needed that jury to like them. It became clear that the "like factor" wasn't always the dispositive factor in a jury's decision, but it was that little extra factor that could make a huge difference in a close call case, which most cases are. The jurors needed to see that lawyer as trustworthy; someone they would like if they ever met outside of the courtroom. It was that little factor that could make a huge difference.

That premise has perhaps never been so clear as it was in the OJ Simpson murder trial. In all of the years that I was a prosecuting attorney, and of all the murder trials I tried, I never had a case with that much overwhelming evidence of guilt. If you ever get a chance to read Vincent Bugliosi's book about this trial, you will be astounded by the clear and convincing evidence that Simpson murdered both his ex-wife and Ron Goldman. There was a problem though. It was the prosecutor. If you watched the case on TV you would have seen lead prosecutor Marcia Clark. She was highly competent, but her competence was overwhelmed by her harsh nature and visibly unlikable personality. A poor job of jury selection set the State up for defeat, but it was enormously enhanced by Clark's lack of demonstrable people skills. Even when she made an effort to be likeable, it was clear that she was trying too hard. It was forced. It was not natural. The jury did not like her. While it may not have been dispositive to the outcome of the case, it made a difference.

The skills I developed after a year of jury observation and work on my own presence in front of people enhanced my advocacy skills, and I was selected as a member of the elite FSU Moot Court Team. This team would compete against top law schools around the country in appellate and trial competitions. By my senior year I was named the Top Oral Trial Advocate by the American Trial Lawyers Association. As a trial lawyer with the state attorney's office, application of these skills translated into a record of 241 jury trials with 232 resulting in conviction.

After ten years in the courtroom, I transitioned my career into business coaching. One of my passions and, in fact, one of my missions in life is to help people understand their full potential and then create a pathway to reach that potential. Over the last twenty-five years, I have worked with thousands of small business owners as well as companies ranging from small start-ups to publically traded companies that generate hundreds of millions of dollars of annual revenue. I have created a methodology that helps companies and individuals assess where they are and create a predictable pathway to the goals they have set for themselves. The last twenty-five years have simply strengthened my belief that cultivating good people skills is the key to success in all areas of life. Without exception, every person I have coached who has made huge progress in his or her business and personal life did so in part by enhancing his or her people skills. This enhancement is a vital piece of the success formula for anyone who is looking to take business or personal performance to the next level.

Now here is the really great news for all readers of this book. People skills are just that: skills that can be learned and improved upon by anyone with the desire to do so. As you read this book, you will learn some basic human interaction lessons that will begin your journey to enhanced people skills. Like almost anything else in life, knowledge is useful only if you put it to use. Each chapter will challenge you to pay close attention to the events of your day and how you and others are interacting with people. There are so many things happening every day that we don't pay attention to because it is simply life unfolding before us. But if you diligently and attentively watch others, you will quickly see that those gaining the most success are those with the best people skills. I am determined to transition you into a person with outstanding people skills. You will value that skill set as one of your greatest personal assets. That skill set will change outcomes in all areas of your life and will open doors that were previously closed.

At the end of each chapter there will be one or more action steps listed. I encourage you to incorporate these action steps into your daily routine. I believe that repetition is the mother of mastery. A simple—and at times subtle—change in personal interaction behavior often produces the most profound results. Also listed are multiple excellent resources to further your education and awareness as you continue your quest to develop enhanced people skills. Each author within these resources has done an exceptional job addressing specific issues that I touch on in this book. And finally, at the end of the book you will find an assessment to help you understand your strengths and weaknesses in relation to awesome people skills. I encourage you to not only take the assessment but to apply as much honesty to your answers as possible.

It is my pleasure to begin your journey to enhanced people skills.

CHAPTER 1

WHY PEOPLE SKILLS ARE THE GREAT DIVIDE

The most important single ingredient in the formula of success is knowing how to get along with people.—Theodore Roosevelt

As you begin your journey to enhanced people skills, I would like to start by asking you a question. Can you think of any skill that influences more areas of your life than people skills? Probably not. Whether you are looking to make a career change, succeed as a spouse or parent, grow a business, deal with a disappointed customer or client, or simply go through life as effectively as possible, how effective you are with people skills will affect every part of your life. While this is certainly not an exhaustive list of areas where people skills have influence, the following will help you understand the vast area of human interaction that they will impact:

Getting a job. When being considered for a job, interpersonal skills trump education, or even experience in the field. According to the International Association of Administrative Professionals (IAAP), people skills are as or more important than experience in a particular field. If you owned a company and your intent was to develop a great company with a great culture, would a candidate's people skill set make a difference to you in the hiring process? Look at job postings. How many say "good people skills necessary"? No one can guarantee you employment for life, but you can stack the deck in your favor—job seekers with a well-developed people skill set are far more employable across an array of industries than those who lack enhanced people skills.

Being promoted. In every profession I have been involved with, it has been an employee's degree of people skills that separated those moving on to bigger and better positions from those left behind. In my experience, where competence is highly important, competence without people skills doesn't deliver the complete package. Let's face a fact: work is competitive and few skills allow you to shine like you can with enhanced people skills. If you were the boss and had two candidates for one promotion, both were close in performance, but one had far greater people skills, who would win?

Becoming a better leader. If you are going to be a leader, people skills are critical. Why? Because leadership is about influence. At its core, leadership has the ability to get other people to perform outside of themselves, beyond where they would perform on their own. For a leader to accomplish this, he or she must bring to the game an array of people skills including effective communication, empathy, and listening. Leadership demands a personality that will inspire action from followers. You rarely see leaders who are hated by those they lead. It is more likely that followers truly like and respect the leader because they know that the leader genuinely cares about them. This earned affection would be impossible without the application of great people skills. Great leaders invariably possess great people skills.

Becoming a better employee. As an employee, you are an ambassador for your company. Customers, clients, and vendors see the company through their experience with you. In today's highly competitive job market, one way to become a more valued and nonexpendable asset to your company is to enhance your people skills. All companies have up and down periods. They have times they are hiring, they have times they are culling the work force based on economic conditions. When you develop great people skills, I assure you that you will increase your likelihood of sticking around, even when times are tough.

Starting a business. As an entrepreneur, I know that starting a successful business has a great deal to do with your degree of people skills. Whether it is hiring new employees, choosing vendors, raising capital, choosing partners, negotiating deals, or pitching your idea and company to customers or investors, if they like you, your chance of success is far greater. If you research any venture capital group and really get behind their decision-making process, you will find that regardless of the merit of the idea, an investment is made in the person first. A venture capital group will fund a C idea with an A person before it funds an A idea with a C person. Few things show more about your values, personality and attitude than your people skills. When starting a business, you will be in the constant state of selling yourself and your concept—people always buy you before they buy your product.

Being an effective partner in a personal relationship. As I write this book, I have just celebrated my thirtieth wedding anniversary. Looking back on this great relationship with the most valued person in my earthly life, I know that being a great listener, compassionate, and bringing a total package of people skills to our relationship has made a huge difference. A successful relationship is a constant flow of back and forth communication and working hard to understand each other. It is about not having to *win* the conversation, but rather *be in* the conversation. That is the essence of good people skills. If you would like to have a highly fulfilling long-term partnership in life, the ability to listen, understand, and interpret communication properly will create the foundation for such a relationship.

Problem solving. This is an area that requires not only analysis but consensus building. I have heard it said that the people who make the most money are the people who solve the biggest problems. While there are certainly problems that can be addressed unilaterally by one person, most problems are addressed and ultimately solved through highly effective analysis, assessment, and an exchange of ideas between all parties involved. Great people skills will help you build consensus and bring out the best ideas from others through your inquisitive listening. They will help you not only solve problems effectively, but empower you to do so in tandem with fellow employees—something every company wants.

Being a great coach or mentor. Most people do not realize that they are already a mentor or coach to one or more family members, friends, or colleagues simply by teaching through daily actions. You and your actions are on display every day. Whether it is your spouse, children, family, or colleagues, people are watching and you are mentoring many more people than you might think—let's call you "the accidental coach." As I mentioned earlier, few things show as much as the people skills that you bring to life. If you are rude on the phone to people, what do your kids see and hear? If you are polite and engaging on the phone, what do they see?

Others take on the role of coach and mentor on purpose. I have been coaching people in business for twenty-five years. Before that, I mentored law interns on trial skills. If someone asked me, "What is the number one trait that makes an effective coach?" my answer would be: people skills. People skills are the key to unlocking a synergistic relationship with another human being; and that can lead to spectacular results. As a coach, you have to know when to push, how far you can push, and you must understand what makes that client tick.

Being a successful parent. I don't know about you, but being a parent (a proud father of three) and seeing kids through the stages of becoming an adult was perhaps my greatest testing ground for effective people skills. If you have negotiated the teenage years, I am sure you will wholeheartedly agree. Effective people skills—including listening, communication, and empathy—will be truly tested as a parent. Children are in a constant state of observing and learning, and the people skills they learn from you will go a long way in determining their trajectory in life. One of my proudest moments came several years ago when I rode with my son to my daughter's wedding. He had a job with a communications company as he was finishing his college education. On this particular drive, my son took several customer calls, and I was blown away by the people skills he brought to those conversations. I thought to myself, "Wow, leading by example really works. I would hire this kid in any company I had because of his awesome people skills."

Being an effective negotiator. If you have ever had to negotiate a deal or contract, you know that the degree of people skills you bring to the bargaining table dictates the outcome. Negotiation done correctly results in a win-win situation for both parties. One of the most powerful aspects of effective people skills is having the ability to give and take in a timely manner. Negotiation is about listening in order to understand what the most important issues are to the person or company you are working with, and if any of these are nonnegotiable.

The great news is that people skills can be learned.

Ten years as a trial lawyer and twenty-five years as a consultant and coach have shown me that not only are good people skills critical to success in any area of life, but they can be vastly improved upon with diligent effort and the specific intent to improve. Literally every person I have ever met who would be considered to have great people skills, developed them over time. The development of great people skills takes time and requires observation, a willingness to be bad until you get good, constant evaluation, and undivided attention paid to your fellow human being.

Working in the restaurant business in college was a great training ground for my early development of people skills. Whether I was waiting tables, tending bar, or running the register, the daily interactions with people demonstrated to me that those who could interact most effectively had the greatest chance of success. Despite the fact that I was serving a hamburger, I quickly learned that McDonald's wasn't a fast-food business; it was a people business that served fast food.

One of my greatest mentors is a gentleman who worked his way up through the ranks of several insurance companies and eventually became the president of Merrill Lynch Insurance. What do you think got him there? Was it because he was an effective salesman and trained others to be like him? Of course, but his success in sales came from the people skills he developed and sharpened over time while sitting at countless kitchen tables with client after client. If you observe this man today, he is a master of people skills. It doesn't matter if the person he is speaking with is wealthy or meager in income. It doesn't matter if the person is outward and bold or withdrawn or shy—he makes everyone feel comfortable and important. Some would call this a gift. I call it a skill developed over many years and tens of thousands of interactions.

My favorite professional golfer is Phil Mickelson, who was inducted into the World Golf Hall of Fame in 2012. At the induction ceremony, the commissioner of the PGA introduced Phil and made some telling comments about who Mickelson is to the golf world. The commissioner commented that he didn't know how much Phil's sponsors paid him, but that because of the exposure Phil brings to their company through his image and unselfish fan-centered attitude, they were not paying him enough. If you have ever watched a golf tournament, you have had the opportunity to observe this genuinely likeable man spend hours signing autographs. But unlike many sports icons, Phil doesn't just sign the paper and hand it back to the adoring fan—he looks in their eyes, flashes his contagious smile, and connects with those fans, furthering his reputation as the world's most popular golfer. There is a reason that he makes far more money off the golf course than on (despite being one of the sport's all-time top money-earners). People love him and know he cares about them. He has enhanced his golf career through the mastery of great people skills.

I am a keen observer of politics. Most politicians have good people skills, but some stand out because of exceptional people skills. Think of a time when you have observed Presidents Kennedy, Clinton, or Obama in a crowd on TV or in a documentary. They always seemed most alive and enjoying their role as president when among the people. A keen observer would admire President George W. Bush and the people skills he brought to the office. If you studied people skills as I do, you would see him as the very best at looking directly into a person's eyes even while progressing along a line of people wanting to get close to him. The next time you see the president walk into Congress to give the State of the Union address, observe whether he simply shakes a hand because it is there or is he connecting eye to eye with that person. President Bush was exceptional at this—if you had watched him at the funerals after September 11, you would have seen a man connecting eye to eye and heart to heart with victims' family members. Each of these accomplished men is comfortable in his own skin—confident and engaging with a dash of humor, a pinch of a timely smile, assertive or self-effacing at the right time. They are all masters of people skills.

In my years of observation, I have found that most people with great people skills developed them through observation and constant application of lessons learned along the way. At a university, classes specific to communications skills are offered, but none specific to people skills, and you are likely to be taught how to talk *at* people, not *with* people. Communication skills, though important, are simply a component of the bigger heading of people skills. Having the ability to talk *at* people is far less impactful than learning how to talk *with* them.

I am convinced that one's daily habits will determine the direction of one's life. A habit I would like to see you put in place in your life is observing others' people skills to note effective and ineffective means of interaction. Have you ever driven to work the same way you have for years and on a particular day you see something new because you just hadn't looked in that spot before? It is the same with observing people skills. Observation is one of the most effective tools you can use to improve your people skills, and when you purposely pay attention, you will note both good and bad people skills.

I have several goals with this book:

First, I want you to realize the importance of people skills in every area of your life.

Second, I want you to be in a constant state of improving your people skills.

Third, I want you to be a keen observer of human behavior. Everyone shows you their people skills or lack thereof every day.

Fourth, I want you to create goals specific to increasing your level of performance relative to your personal people skills.

Fifth, I want you to be accountable to someone you respect and have them observe your people skills as you work on improving them.

Finally, my intent is for you to become hungry to learn more about people skills from other authors. In that vein, I will introduce you to a reading list at the end of each chapter that I believe will be helpful for you as you begin your journey to enhanced people skills. I would also love for you to tell me stories of your successes, failures, and improvements by sending an e-mail along your journey to john@johnterhune.com

When you combine and refine empathy, great listening skills, humor, a well-read intellect, an inquisitive personality, a genuine smile, a steel-trap memory for names, and a heartfelt interest in other people, you are on your way to greater success in every area of your life.

Action Steps:

1. Become a keen observer of people skills demonstrated by those around you.

2. Identify specific areas of people skills in which you need to improve.

3. Create an accountability relationship with someone whom you respect and who has great people skills. Ask them to observe you in action and give you an honest evaluation.

4. Take the People Skills Assessment at www.johnterhune.com/peopleskills

Recommended Resources:

People First, by Jack Lannom; http://www.thinkpeoplefirst.com/

Attitude Pump 110—You Improve What You Measure, by John Terhune; www.johnterhune.com/attitude

CHAPTER 2

WHY PEOPLE BUY YOU BEFORE THEY BUY YOUR PRODUCT

All things being equal, people will do business with, and refer business to, those people they know, like, and trust.—Bob Burg, Wallstreet Journal and Business Week best selling author

In my introduction I wrote about the discovery I made regarding jury trial work and case presentation before a jury. If the jury liked me they would be far more likely to listen to my arguments favorably. That was a profound lesson in my young life as an aspiring trial lawyer and it paid huge dividends as I launched a career as a prosecuting attorney for the State of Florida. Since many of the cases I would "sell" to the jury would be close calls, I knew that anything that I could do to help them like me would make a difference.

In the jurisdiction where I tried a vast majority of my 200-plus cases, the jury pool was assembled in a large courtroom. Most potential jurors would arrive early to await being called into the jury box and questioned by the lawyers—a process known as *voir dire* (French for "to tell the truth"). Knowing that most of the jurors were in a new environment and thus highly observant of the goings on in the courtroom, I made it a practice to also arrive early.

Once I put my briefcase at my table, I would immediately walk over and converse with the courtroom personnel. I'd shake the bailiff's hand and talk for a moment, share a laugh, then depart with a pat on the back as a gesture of friendship. I did the same with both the court reporter and court clerk. The potential jurors were far enough away that they could not hear us, but they could tell that these working people of the courtroom liked me and felt comfortable in my presence. Subtly, I was planting in the observing juror's mind that this is a likeable guy who I (the juror) would like if I met him outside of the courtroom. Part of the exchange with the court personnel always included laughter and smiles and, importantly, questions about them and their family. When you express genuine interest in someone else's life, that person can engage more fully in a conversation. You also endear yourself to that person through your interest.

Now this may sound as though I was using the court personnel to my advantage. Not at all. These were not superficial exchanges. I had been building those relationships for years by delivering my wife's homemade holiday food gifts to the sheriff's, court reporter's, and clerk's offices; remembering the names of husbands, wives, kids; remembering birthdays; and inquiring about ongoing health problems. These court personnel were used to arrogant attorneys viewing them as mere employees of the court system; I went out of my way to make them feel special and appreciated.

When the judge called twelve potential jurors from the audience to be questioned by first the judge and then the attorneys, he would direct all twelve into a jury box in the front of the courtroom. The judge would always ask the jurors a series of questions to determine their initial qualifications to sit as jurors. That process usually took about ten minutes.

While the judge was questioning the potential jurors, I was memorizing their names. I knew when the defense lawyer had an opportunity to question each juror, he would have to refer to a written list in order to address each juror. As I questioned the jurors, I had no paper with me—I addressed each one by name.

Again, a subtle but powerful way to communicate that I cared enough to know them by name, and that each of them was important enough for me to remember their name. One of the greatest skills you will develop within your enhanced people skills is the ability to remember names long after an initial introduction. A person's name is their identity—by taking the time to recognize people by name, not only do you tell them they are significant, but you are remembered as standing out from the crowd.

Typically, I had only about five minutes to question a juror before making my decision about their service on this particular jury. Each lawyer had a certain number of preemptory challenges where he or she could strike the juror from the list for no stated reason. This colloquy between me and the potential juror provided yet another opportunity to further their "like" of me. The questions were similar, so it was the subtleties of the five-minute exchange that would make the difference. I knew the jurors were nervous, but if I could put them at ease and make it a pleasant experience, my cause would be once again well served. Doing so became an art form for me. I combined genuine eye contact, smiles at the appropriate times, body language that said I was listening to them, respectful language and, most importantly, listening skills that allowed me to hear exactly what they were saying. Many trial lawyers tend to be canned in their questioning of jurors, but I always wanted to have a conversation with the juror and respond to them with questions that said, "I heard what you just said." People want to be heard. People want to be listened to. By doing so you are telling them that they matter, that they are significant.

By the time jury selection was over, my first goal in the courtroom that day was achieved—the jurors liked me. If human beings like each other, they have taken the first step toward trusting each other. While this methodology didn't work every time, it did result in my winning 97 percent of my jury trials. The challenge of persuading twelve people to reach a unanimous decision is daunting, but I approached it utilizing these subtle yet vital people skills I had been developing for years.

The premise of this chapter is that people buy you before they buy your product. Or said another way: people buy from people they like. The last time you bought an automobile from a dealership, did you "buy" the salesman before you bought the car? If I want to buy a car and the salesperson is a jerk, there are other dealerships in the area that I will take my business to before I buy from that salesperson. In fact, I would drive out of my way to buy the same car if I wasn't treated right by the salesperson. If I do not like you, there is no way I am going to spend that kind of money through you. When I buy a car, I have to buy the salesman before I buy the car.

Recently, my wife and I purchased long-term care insurance. We met with the insurance agent for coffee and to discuss the policy. If I had not liked him, I wouldn't have purchased the policy; there are plenty of agents that sell the same policy from the same company. I had to know he wasn't just selling a policy but was offering a solution that considered all of my circumstances, and would be on my side if any issues arose. I had to know that he cared, that he would be my advocate, that I would be more than a numbered policy, and that I would be treated as a valued friend whom he would match with the best policy for my needs. He was exactly what we wanted. This man listened far more than he talked. When he did talk it was to ask questions so that he could match us with the right product. Even before we got into the insurance side of our conversation, we spoke for more than an hour getting to know one another. He understood that we had to buy him before we were going to buy any policy, and for us to buy him we had to like him. That meant that he had to bring good people skills to the conversation.

If you were to follow the path of the most successful business people, you would find out that their customers are more than just customers—they are valued relationships. People don't create valued relationships with people they don't like. To distinguish yourself in the marketplace in this time of brutal competition, you have to remember something about business: No business is a product business first. It is a people business first. When you bring great people skills to your business and life, you will be liked by more people including your customers. When people like you, they are willing to buy from you. If they don't like you, they will find somewhere else to spend their money. Would you buy something from someone who was not fully engaged in listening to your needs and helping you meet them?

One of the most effective ways to make people like you is to express genuine appreciation. In her June 2013 article in *Forbes* magazine entitled "People Do Business With People They Like," entrepreneur, CEO, mentor, and speaker Amy Rees Anderson says it best:

> *People ultimately choose to do business with people they like, and everyone likes someone who appreciates them. I once read a quote by the ever so brilliant writer known as Anonymous. It states that "people forget what you said. People forget what you did. But people will never forget how you made them feel." The most powerful tool you have in creating success in your life is to appreciate other people.*

I can't begin to tell you how true I have found this statement to be in my personal and professional life. The average person takes people for granted because their focus is on themselves. For decades, I have gone out of my way to express gratitude to people in both my personal and professional lives.

Have you had a boss assign a project to you but never express gratitude for your obvious effort to get it done and done well? Did you receive anything other than superficial gratitude since "it was your job" to serve that person? How did that make you feel? Does that behavior inspire loyalty and respect? On the other hand, have you had a boss who recognized your extra effort on a project, expressed genuine gratitude for a job well done, mentioned your work to colleagues, and commented what an asset you are to the company? For whom would you rather work? The genuine expression of appreciation will make you stand out from the crowd.

This concept was never so clearly demonstrated in my professional life as when I was a trial lawyer. Many attorneys have great people skills, but the practice of law tends to attract an inordinate number of arrogant people, and the vast majority of lawyers see court personnel as their servants. It was amazing to see court staff practically glow when I went out of my way to compliment them and show appreciation for their work. I cannot tell you how many times over a decade-long career trying cases that those people went out of their way to help me. I even had a signal worked out with the bailiffs to let me know what the verdict was before it was read in the courtroom. The bailiff ferried communication between the judge and jury—he or she would hear the knock on the door indicating a question or verdict and then would communicate that to the judge. Finally, the jurors would reach a verdict and the bailiff would see the verdict form before the jury entered the courtroom—a jingle of courthouse keys signaled a conviction.

Numerous times the defendant, while being escorted from a holding cell, would make a casual statement that would help me in the case and a deputy sheriff would pass it on to me. Why? Because he liked me. He liked me because I treated him with respect and dignity and I expressed appreciation to him for a job well done. I knew his situation in life because I took the time to speak with him and listen genuinely to his issues. He knew I cared. I don't care what business you are in, human beings have to buy you before they buy your product. The only way for them to buy you is to like you, and the only way for them to like you is to for you to show them that you care about them; that they are important to you. Not because of what you can leverage from them, but what you can gain as a person from having a friendship with them.

Deal's Famous Oyster House is a restaurant outside of Perry, Florida. Every time a patron walks through the front door, one of the employees says loudly, "The finest people in the world walk through that door every day. Welcome to Deal's!" For decades this restaurant has maintained a loyal patronage in the same small town because their customers knows that announcement is more than a slogan—it is a way of doing business. People like the owner and employees and the attention paid to them as loyal patrons of Deal's.

If you are a small company or sole proprietor, this concept of people liking you before they do business with you should make perfect sense. If you work for a large company, there may be hundreds or thousands of "touch points" where the potential customer has the opportunity to like or dislike the company and thus express that sentiment through engaging (or not) in business with you. That is exactly why people skills are such a vital area of training for employees in all departments of a company. At any touch point between a company and a customer, you must have people with enhanced people skills to advance your image, mission, and vision in a way that will get your customers to like you. Allow me to give you an example:

I once called a toll-free number prompted by the offer of a free CD demonstrating the ease of learning a foreign language with a particular company. When I called, the operator taking the call would not send me the CD as requested, but rather went into a high pressure sales mode seeking to sell me their program. Within minutes of engaging on the phone, I disliked this company. The company told me one thing, but did another. Because of that experience, I sought another solution. It may have had the best product, but I did not buy it because I did not like the business method of saying one thing and then doing another. If you want people to like you, it would be wise to do what you say. In business, *like* equals *trust*—if they don't like you, they won't trust you; and if they don't trust you, they won't like you.

Within the last several months, I took my BMW in for service. Because it is out of the fifty-thousand-mile warranty period, I take it to a gentleman who works exclusively on foreign cars. The issue with my car had to do with the fuel pump, and fixing it through him would have cost well over $500. However, he did some research and learned that particular part had been recalled (I had received no notice from BMW), and that if I contacted the BMW dealership where I bought the car, they would most likely replace the pump because of the recall. That advice cost my mechanic hundreds of dollars at that moment. But not really. I have recommended him to dozens of people because he is an honest mechanic. I wouldn't think of taking my car anywhere else because I know he is watching out for me first. By putting me first, he generated more money than if he had gone for the quick $500.

In business, there are many ways to stand out and have the potential customer like you. Here is a list to act as a reminder and a measuring tool for your intention of being liked as a business person.

1. Do what you say. Trust is slowly earned and rapidly lost. Make this a foundational habit of life and business dealings. When people trust you, it is easier for them to like you.

2. View every customer experience as a building block toward a long-term relationship. Companies and people who view business as merely a transaction are shortsighted and usually short-lived. Smart people and companies view each transaction as one in a long line of transactions designed to enrich the life and experience of the customer who has chosen to do business with you. Making a customer feel valued well after the transaction is gold to a business owner.

3. Learn and live by the concept of underselling and overdelivering. People or companies that inflate their value set themselves up to disappoint customers. By underpromising and overdelivering, the customer always comes away from the transaction feeling wowed.

4. Regardless of the superior nature of your product or service, always express confidence in what you offer without slamming another brand or competitor. If your product or service is that good it will speak for itself and distinguish itself from the competition. Your respectful dealing with another brand or competitor will gain respect from your customer.

5. Be willing to point your customer to another source if it has the best solution for your customer's needs. A business that cares enough to point me to another resource will win my loyalty because I know that I am more to them than this single transaction.

6. Become an expert in whatever business you represent. That means understanding the marketplace beyond your own product. Understand the competition. Understand emerging technologies specific to your business. Customers like to consult an expert who will create ease and confidence in their buying decision.

Action Steps:

1. When dealing with potential customers, go out of your way to keep your or your company's word, and make them feel that they are the most important part of your relationship. Make them feel valued beyond their economic impact.

2. Watch people around you who are clearly liked, and identify how they treat their patrons and what things they do to make that relationship special.

Recommended Resources:

The 11 Laws of Likability, by Michelle Tillis Lederman; www.michelletillislederman.com

Attitude Pump 154—An Attitude of Delivering Excellence, by John Terhune; www.johnterhune.com/attitude

The Go Giver by Bob Burg and John David Mann; www.thegogiverway.com

CHAPTER 3

A GREAT SELF-IMAGE: THE BEGINNING OF GREAT PEOPLE SKILLS

There is overwhelming evidence that the higher the level of self-esteem, the more likely one will be to treat others with respect, kindness, and generosity.—Nathaniel Branden

Your ability to enhance your people skills will be highly dependent on the image that you have of yourself. The first step in enhancing your people skills is to enhance your self-image.

After my study of thousands of human beings and the ways that they interact with other humans, I am more convinced than ever before that the degree of your people skills will be highly dependent on your self-image. The reason this is true is that people with a great self-image don't have to win the conversation. They don't need to prove anything. Conversations and interactions can be focused on the other person instead of themselves.

Self-image is the way you view yourself. It incorporates every event, decision, interaction, thought, and outcome in your life. Here is an easy way to look at self-image: Imagine that you are driving your car down the road of life. As you look in the rearview mirror you see every event of your life. Each day that you live there is another day's worth of decisions about hundreds of issues, commitments you fulfilled or didn't fulfill, promises you kept or broke, the self-discipline you did or did not exercise, things you did when others weren't looking or listening, statements you made whether they were uplifting or damaging, human interactions be they good or bad, all becoming a part of that picture in the rearview mirror. In my experience, a person will never outperform for any extended period of time their personal self-image. Have you ever seen someone gain temporary success only to crash and burn within a short period of time? If you looked behind the circumstances, you would have seen that the person did not have the self-image needed to sustain the level of performance or success that had been temporarily gained.

Visiting the other side of the self-image spectrum, have you seen people whose inflated self-image was their downfall? You know those people who feel and demonstrate through their actions that they are superior and that other people exist to serve their needs. Remember the words of Carly Simon: "You're so vain, I bet you think this song is about you." Have you engaged in conversations with people who could not stop talking about themselves? It takes an inner confidence to project an outer humility. If you listen to the most successful people in life, you will find they have a humble spirit and are much quicker to talk about someone else rather than themselves. That reflects a deep inner confidence that they know who they are and that their actions speak louder than their words.

We all know egotistical people. These people's inflated view of themselves is much like a strutting peacock and destroys their ability to leverage the potential found within a great people skill set. It turns out that most of these people actually have a poor self-image and are overcompensating for a lack of self-confidence by putting out a false persona that inflates the way they truly view themselves. People with great self-images don't need to rule the conversation, and they don't take up a lot of oxygen in the room the way people with inflated self-images do.

People with a great self-image don't need to falsely inflate themselves beyond who they are in their mind's eye. They have a natural ease that makes them easy to be around. People with a good self-image make conversations about the other person, not about themselves. They don't need to prove anything. They are self-effacing and humble. They don't need to win the conversation; they are simply fully engaged in it. They smile with sincerity and make the other person feel better about themselves. People with great self-images have the foundation for great people skills. Everyone every day is building up or damaging their self-image. It is a never-ending human process that you have control over if you are paying attention. Let's talk about a number of areas where you can dramatically improve your self-image.

Understand that you are writing the history of your life every day. Your history is being written by your actions and decisions every single day. Knowing that you are in the process of writing the history of your life, it is time to make quality decisions and take quality actions that are deeply rooted in character, integrity, and self-discipline. This course of action will, over time, build the pride factor in your life. I call it the "I am proud of me" factor. When you can look in the rearview mirror and see the history of your life and be proud of yourself, then your self-image will be spectacular.

How you feel about yourself physically impacts your self-image. When I feel fit, when my clothes are loose instead of tight, I am a different person than when I feel overweight, and my pants are digging into my waist. I absolutely know that I interact with people in a different way when I don't feel good about my physical appearance. When I feel lean and in shape, I tend to respond instead of react. My tolerance of other people is much higher when I am in great shape. What about for you?

Do you feel more confident and at ease when you are at exactly the weight you should be and your clothes fit correctly? Part of having great people skills is being at ease in all circumstances of human interaction. Physical appearance and how you feel about yourself is a huge piece of the self-image puzzle. The good news is that this is an area over which you have complete control. Maintaining great physical conditioning is an exercise of self-discipline every day.

As I write this book, I have just turned sixty years young. Knowing that I would turn sixty, I began this year with a personal battle cry: *Better in every way.* I have been exercising regularly for forty years; still, one of the ways that I needed to get better had to do with my physical conditioning. As I began the year, I wasn't totally out of shape—I wasn't totally in shape either—but I was about twenty pounds over my ideal weight. I completely changed the way I eat, and decided for the first time in my life to become a morning person. I arrive at the YMCA every morning at seven, work on my core strength for an hour, followed by an intense fifty-minute spin class with a trainer who pushes me to the edge. This self-discipline over the year has resulted in my losing twenty pounds and four inches off my waist. I weigh less now than I did when I was thirty-five, and everywhere I go, people comment on how great I look. At my annual physical, my doctor was very impressed with my outstanding blood work.

Now here is the important part of this story: I had a great self-image before I improved my health and appearance, but now I have enhanced my self-image through self-discipline in eating and exercising. I feel a greater ease in my interaction other people. A year ago, if you had observed me you would have thought, "That guy has phenomenal people skills." However, by upping my game when it came to my physical appearance, I upped my self-image and thus set a pathway to even better people skills. I feel great in my skin. When you feel like that, you subconciously braodcast that to other people, making it easy and enjoyable for others to be around you.

A regimen of physical exercise is one of the most important ingredients in developing a great self-image. Beyond the tremendous self-image boost that you get when you are physically fit, there is an equally if not more important aspect of a regimen of physical exercise: the mental fitness that comes as the result of exercising self-discipline and your "I refuse to quit" muscle. The application of these two mental ingredients will lead to a great self-image. Implementing a daily regimen of healthy eating habits will lead to a greater self-image. You get fat one meal at a time, just as you will get lean one meal at a time. It takes day after day application of self-discipline and a healthy eating strategy to reach fitness and weight goals. A key habit to develop is to get as much pleasure from the application of self-discipline as you do from the temporary pleasure of indulgence.

Self-discipline is one of the greatest ways to enhance your self-image. If you look in your rearview mirror and see a person who always opts for the easy way and does not apply self-discipline to life, it is going to be very difficult to feel good about yourself. Self-discipline is all about delayed gratification. Self-discipline is a muscle and a habit that will become the foundation for a great self-image. Delayed gratification is a manifestation of taking a long-term view of the event that presents the choice of instant vs. delayed gratification. Instant gratification doesn't take self-discipline—it just takes giving in! Delayed gratification exercised over time will actually allow you to feel instant gratification as the result of the exercise of self-discipline in the moment. Instant gratification is easy. It is immediate. It is what the masses will choose most of the time. When you begin to implement delayed gratification and implementing self-discipline you will in time enhance your self-image and thus enhance your foundation for great people skills.

Your daily language creates a pathway to an enhanced self-image. An encouraging word and an uplifting attitude expressed to another human being have the potential to change a day or even a life. Because negative language is so pervasive, you will stand out if you exhibit an uplifting encouraging attitude through your language. Language from your mouth reflects the attitude in your heart. As you stand up for your principles, you will feel great about yourself and create a greater degree of self-respect, thus improving your self-image. Your language sends a message to the world regarding who you are. Use language that makes you feel good about yourself. Use language that makes you proud of you. Remember, your brain is always hearing what you are saying. Positive spoken is positive heard. A genuine encouragement to another human being is like you putting her on your shoulders and lifting her over the wall on the obstacle course of life.

Now, remember that rearview mirror. You know how you spoke to people yesterday. You know if your words empowered them or discouraged them. How good do you feel when you make someone smile through your words? How bad do you feel if your words leave another person injured? There are times when words are far more powerful than any physical weapon; the scars of hurtful words remain for years, sometimes a lifetime. The same can be said for positive words that lift people up, give them hope, and make them feel great. Those positive uplifting words may have made the difference in that person's life. I have a simple rule: any time I have a conversation with someone, I want to leave them feeling better than before we engaged in that conversation.

How are you viewed by the people who know you best? To me, one of the greatest measures of who you are as a person, and thus how you see yourself, is the degree of heartfelt respect you have from the family members who live with the real you. People tend to play roles in the business world. The outside world never sees the real you as clearly as family members do. A great way to have a spectacular self-image is to know in your heart that the people who know you the best, respect you the most. That is when you deserve a terrific self-image and when you will have the strongest foundation for great people skills.

How well do you perform on your bad days? Anyone can perform well on their good days. Life is all about how well you perform on the days you are not at your best. Even on days when you may be tired, your attitude can assist you in achieving excellent results even when you don't feel like performing at a level of excellence. How well you perform on bad days is a greater measure of the results that you will get in life than how you perform when you are feeling good. The right attitude will help you outperform how you feel.

How easily are you discouraged? Over several decades working with people seeking success, I have been amazed at how low the threshold is for most people when it comes to becoming discouraged. If you look in the rearview mirror and see a person who makes a run at something only to lose interest and passion along the way, it is almost impossible to have a great self-image. Quitting or not quitting happens as the result of the muscle that you build over time that either gives into or defeats the voice in your head looking for the path of least resistance. When you build a strong "never quit" muscle, it will activate in all areas of your life. When you get an "I will never quit" attitude that is supported by an "I will never quit" muscle, you are well on your way to winning in all aspects of your life. Nobody bursts onto the scene as a success; it is a process that takes years. If you are willing to pursue your vision with passion until you win, then you are way ahead of those who are easily discouraged before they put in enough effort to be in a position to win.

How consistent are you in all areas of your life? Have you ever been inconsistent in your exercise, relationships, work ethic, vision, or moods? Did you notice that inconsistency leads to predictably poor results? A secret of the most successful people is the application of consistency in all areas of life, particularly with your attitude. The minute you allow the circumstances of life to affect the consistency of your attitude, you will dramatically affect the potential of your win in life.

Are you living a life grounded in integrity? Integrity is a reflection of one's character. Character is the culmination of one's morals and values. A character that reflects a consistent application of integrity leaves a long-term impression on your self-image and the people who are watching you in life. When you live a life that is underscored with integrity, your actions and words become so powerful that they can become the example for others to emulate

How do you handle adversity? The average person does not understand the value of adversity. It is not a matter of whether you face adversity on the way to success; it is a matter of how you handle it and how it affects your attitude. Most successful people in life have failed multiple times on the way to their victory. If you had occasion to interview most highly successful people, they would tell you that their failures taught them more than their victories. They used the failures and the lessons within the failure as fertilizer for their future victories. Adversity makes you dig down within yourself to find out what you are really made of—how you handle it will help you achieve what your goals.

Are you mission or money driven? People whose lives are driven by mission rather than money tend to feel better about themselves and have a greater self-image. Isn't there something inside of you that you know you are capable of that you are not currently pursuing with all of your passion? Isn't there something you can do to serve humankind that will ultimately serve you and those you love? Would you like your eulogy to say something more than you were very good at providing a nice living for your family?

There is within each of us a potential that few ever reach. Most never get there because of their unwillingness to take action and leave their safe harbor. Spend ten minutes in the presence of a person who is being driven by a mission beyond earning a paycheck—in that person you will see a profound self-confidence, an attitude that survives exhaustion, a glow in her eyes reflecting an optimistic heart, and an expectation level that touches all areas of her life. You will see within her the power and effect of deep-seated meaning. In that person you will see a human being who is truly alive, creating an amazing view in her rearview mirror that becomes the foundation for a spectacular self-image.

Measure yourself by who you are becoming, not by what you are achieving. If you concentrate on *becoming* instead of *achieving*, achieving will happen. Said another way, the journey is every bit as important as the desitination. If for example you are aiming to become the CEO of your company, the fastest pathway there is to become the person you need to become through experience and personal self development to be the logical choice for the position. By working on you first, you put yourself in the position to achieve your desired results. If you can grow as a person by an inch a day then those inches become feet, then a yard, then a mile, finally adding up to a marathon of personal growth, you can achieve anything that your heart desires.

How effective are you at getting things done on time? Get into a habit of listing five things you must get done each day that will progress you toward your goals. Many people spend a day being busy, but not productive. But just five accomplishments each day add up to thousands over the year. It is difficult to have a great self-image when your rearview mirror view is cluttered with things left undone.

Action Steps:
1. Develop an action plan to get in physical shape by combining exercise, eating, and self-discipline.
2. Pay close attention to the words you are using when conversing with other people. Are they encouraging and uplifting? Do people appear to feel better about themselves after your conversation?
3. View all areas of your life and determine where you are inconsistent in your efforts and apply consistent self-discipline in that area from now on.

4. Identify any areas in your life you could improve upon and put an action plan in place to do just that.

Recommended Resources:

Success and the Self-Image, by Zig Ziglar; www.ziglar.com

Attitude Pump 122—The "I Am Proud of Me" Factor, by John Terhune; www.johnterhune.com/attitude

CHAPTER 4

PEOPLE WANT TO BE APPRECIATED AND RESPECTED

The deepest principle in human nature is the craving to be appreciated.—William James

One of the most important arrows in your enhanced people skills quiver is understanding the powerful human responses you will motivate when you show people true appreciation and respect. A theme throughout this book is that as a consequence of your great people skills, people will be far more inclined to like you. They will like being with you. They will like conversing with you. They will feel good about introducing you to their friends or family. They will not feel threatened by you. They will feel safe in your presence. Few things can do that as effectively as conveying that you are a confident, humble person who genuinely appreciates and respects others.

There is perhaps no personal characteristic that evokes trust and like better than humility. People who are humble are confident as human beings. The focus doesn't need to be on them—they know who they are without having to project it onto another person. It is the self-confident, humble person who is most capable of showing respect and appreciation to someone else. Respect means showing regard and appreciation for the worth of someone or something. Respect means honoring another person's wants, needs, ideas, differences, beliefs, customs, and heritage. Respect means using good manners by being courteous and polite, speaking to others in a kind voice, and using polite body language. Respecting others begins with respecting yourself. Swiss philosopher Henri-Frédéric Amiel said it well: "Respect is most easily given by the quietly confident person who is based in humility. There is no respect for others without humility in one's self."

One of the greatest ways to show respect is by listening. By listening well to another person, you are saying: I respect what you say and how you feel so much that I am not going to talk, but rather listen completely to what you are saying.

People with enhanced people skills are even able to disagree with respect. If I am ever in a conversation with another person and I disagree with them, I always preface my comments by saying, "I respectfully disagree with your position," and then respectfully articulate my position. Being a trial lawyer, I love the art of debate done well. If you would like to see the art of debate done poorly, watch any cable news channel with two "experts" debating an issue. How many times do you see one talk over or interrupt the other—or even resort to name-calling—all to win the debate? In my mind, that person has lost the debate, regardless of their position, because all I can hear is the total lack of respect shown for the other person. People with enhanced people skills understand how to disagree in a respectful manner.

It is always a pleasure to watch and listen to two people have a civil debate while demonstrating respect for each other, despite their conflicting positions. Once upon a time, politics was an art of people skills.

Once upon a time, politicians would fight like dogs on the floor of Congress only to spend the evening having a friendly dinner or drink together. Some of the greatest and most effective legislation resulted from a House of Representatives led by Democrat Tip O'Neil and Republican President Ronald Reagan. These men came from opposite sides of the ideological fence, yet they worked effectively together to change the direction of our country's economy. That was possible because debates over issues were conducted with civility and respect. Unfortunately, by all appearances, those days of civil discord and respectful disagreement are a thing of the past. What was once "The statement by the senator is disingenuous," is now "The senator is a liar." A show of respect opens the ears. A show of disrespect slams the ears and the heart shut.

Before you finish this book, you will have a good feel for how important I believe daily habits are in leading an extraordinary life. I think one of the best you could add to your life is being more cognizant of people and finding ways to share words of appreciation and respect for their efforts. Sometimes a small amount of appreciation will be the exact thing a person needed to help navigate a tough day. In reading this book, you will become very familiar with my belief that it is easy to separate yourself from the masses and be seen as extraordinary by making a daily conscious effort to separate your actions in every aspect of your life from that of the average person. A genuine and effective show of appreciation and respect will make you stand out like an oasis in the desert.

In my years as a prosecuting attorney or a business coach, I've never met a person who felt overappreciated. In fact, it is usually exactly the opposite. In my experience, a proper dose of praise and appreciation unleashes a willingness to go the extra mile. Integrity-based people will always go out of their way to return the kindness felt through your appreciation and respect. By their nature, people are going to dig deeper, try harder, and work longer when they know you appreciate their efforts. Great leaders express appreciation—they know people are willing to take extra action when a leader appreciates their effort and heart. A vital part of being an effective leader is getting your followers to perform beyond their norm and reach that zone achieved only by a following a leader's inspiration.

One of the most effective ways to show true appreciation is to compose a short, handwritten note. You've had a really bad day, but in your mail is a note of thanks and appreciation for a task well done. How good would that make you feel? Would you go out of your way to help that person who sent the note? Investing the little bit of time it takes to compose a handwritten note will separate your actions from those of others. How many e-mails have you saved? How many handwritten notes have you saved? Appreciation is valuing something highly and showing gratitude. A handwritten note memorializes that sentiment.

President Reagan was famous for his handwritten letters expressing his appreciation. It was a handwritten letter to the American people in which he announced that he had Alzheimer's disease. A wonderful insight into this president can be found in the great read, *Reagan: A Life in Letters.*

There are times when a simple compliment can make someone's day. The well-timed, sincere compliment is another form of showing appreciation. Mark Twain was famous for saying that "I can live for two months on a good compliment." I make a habit of complimenting people on their choice of clothing color. You would be amazed by how people glow after me saying something as simple as "That color really suits you." The key to giving someone a compliment is that it must be genuine. Compliments make other people feel good—it boosts their self-esteem and gives them warm feelings toward you.

Action Steps:

1. Show appreciation to both your colleagues and family members.
2. Give a compliment to someone who appears to be having a bad day.
3. When your opinion differs from someone else's, show respect for his position while respectfully disagreeing with him.

Recommended Resources:

The 5 Languages of Appreciation in the Workplace: Empowering Organizations by Encouraging People, by Gary D. Chapman and Paul E. White; www.5lovelanguages.com

Attitude Pump 113—An Attitude of Gratitude, by John Terhune; www. johnterhune.com/attitude

CHAPTER 5

HOW WELL DO YOU LISTEN?

Most people do not listen with the intent to understand; they listen with the intent to reply. They're either speaking or preparing to speak. They're filtering everything through their own paradigms, reading their autobiography into other people's lives.—Stephen Covey, best selling author

Hearing and listening are very different. Hearing is about sounds. Listening is about intentional focus. Listening means paying attention to not only what is being said, but the use of language, tone of voice, and body language—being aware of both verbal and nonverbal communication. Your ability to listen well depends on the degree to which you perceive and understand these various forms of communication from one human being to another.

When I was a trial lawyer, it was the norm to go home after a full day exhausted, with a splitting headache. I had spent the day listening intently to every word spoken and watching every action taken by each witness. As a trial lawyer, I was trained to listen for inconsistencies in testimony or that unintentional stumble by a witness that might open the door to attack his credibility. I went home exhausted because listening is hard work: Hearing is passive. Listening is active. I was not only hearing what the witness said, I was listening to the way he or she said it, and watching their body language. Emotions aren't expressed solely in words; they are expressed through the eyes, hands, body, and face. The human being is a complex, integrated machine that speaks with different parts in every conversation.

There is no doubt that my training as a trial lawyer vastly improved my listening skills, which in turn enhanced my overall people skills. In fact, being a great listener is at the top of my list of required great people skills—it is the pathway to engaging people in true conversation and dialogue, and a pathway to the heart of another human being. When you reach the heart of that person, you will find another level of human communication critical to great people skills. You will enter the land of the relationship where that person will trust you. It is the pathway to someone liking you because you care about them. Unfortunately, listening is practically a forgotten art—people are so busy talking that they forget to listen.

The good news is that listening is a skill that can be developed with intentional practice. I say intentional practice because to really improve in this area you must have a very *specific intent* to improve. A specific intent to improve leads to ongoing personal assessment of your skill set. A general intent results in skipping the necessary step in true and effective skill set enhancement: ongoing self-assessment. At the end of this book, you will be able to take an assessment of your people skills, and will note that a substantial portion of the questions address your listening skills.

So let's talk about being a great listener. If you were the proverbial "fly on the wall" while I was talking to someone, you would observe me employing multiple skills during that conversation. You would observe a great listener. The first step in enhancing your listening skills is simply deciding to become a great listener. As in many things in life, a quality decision to change or improve is the primary and fundamental step that leads to improvement. Having an underlying reason to improve something makes the decision to do so easier. According to Bernard Ferrari, author of _Power Listening: Mastering the Most Critical Business Skill of All,_ "good listening is the key to developing fresh insights and ideas that fuel success."

Adults spend an average of 70 percent of their time engaged in some sort of communication. Of this, experts tell us that an average of 45 percent is spent listening, 30 percent speaking, 16 percent reading, and 9 percent writing. I guarantee that making a quality decision to become a great listener is going to impact every aspect of your life. Once the quality, no turning back decision has been made let's get down to the mechanics of being a great listener so you begin implementation into every conversation.

What does it take to become a great listener?

There is no one thing that will transition you into a great listener. It starts with the decision to become a better listener, followed by specific intent every day. Being a great listener requires an orchestration of the senses and a overall engagement with the person to whom you are listening. It requires the specific intent to not simply hear what is being said, but to listen to what is being said. Hearing requires the engagement of your ears. Listening requires the engagement of your ears, heart, body, and mind. Below I have listed the attributes of a great listener. The more of these you engage while listening, the more effective listener you will be.

Demonstrate genuine interest in the person and in the subject of the conversation. People can tell when someone is just "going through the motions" in a conversation. Few things are more insulting than when the person I am talking to does not pay attention to what we are

talking about. Genuine interest can be expressed in many ways, from your body language to the quality of your questions. The key word here is genuine; feigned interest is as bad as or even worse than no interest.

Listen without formulating a response. Have you ever been in a conversation with someone and caught yourself thinking about what to say next? When you do that, you aren't fully engaged in listening. Make a conscious effort to listen to everything being said through words and body language, and then formulate your response. One of the greatest lessons I learned as a trial lawyer was to trust the speed of my brain and its ability to remember. I was famous for not taking notes during the trail as I was intently listening to the testimony. Writing while listening thwarted my abililty to completely listen. I assure you that your brain will produce a great response *after* listening to all that is said.

Don't try to beat their story. How many times has someone told you a story and you had what you considered to be a similar but greater experience and you just couldn't wait for him to finish so that you could tell your better story on the same subject? Having traveled extensively around the world over the last quarter of a century it is rare that I can't top any story someone will tell me about their travel experiences. I nonetheless refrain from doing so. You may in fact have an area or multiple areas in your life that give you the ability to win with your experiences and story. Guard against doing so if you want to be considered a great listener.

Engage your mental and physical being in the conversation. Your body language speaks volumes about your level of genuine interest. Leaning forward at the right moment; making appropriate eye contact; nodding, smiling, agreeing, or laughing at appropriate times; and not checking your phone are all part of an orchestration of body and mind that says you are genuinely interested in the conversation.

Ask intelligent and pertinent questions that continue the flow of the conversation. It's also important to note that asking respectful questions does not mean that they can't be tough or pointed. The key is to ask in a manner that will help, not hinder, the free and open flow of communication and idea generating. Engage the person by asking questions that show your genuine interest.

Don't talk over the other person. Have you ever had a conversation with someone who constantly interrupted or talked over you? That person is telling you that she is not listening, that she thinks what she has to say is more important, and that she doesn't care what you have to say.

Listen to their body language. There is no greater way to tell someone you are listening to them than engaging your body language in the conversation. That doesn't mean being overly engaged. It means that your body language tells them that what he or she is saying is important and that you are genuinely interested.

Follow up at a later time after reflecting on what was said. One of the greatest ways to tell someone that you have listened to them is to bring the conversation up at a later date, telling them how much you enjoyed speaking with them. You can drive the point home by asking a question of them based on that conversation, such as, "Jim, you really got me thinking the other day when we were speaking."

It will be easy to tell if you're becoming a good listener—just see how many people want to engage in conversation with you. One of the greatest compliments you will ever receive is that you are a great listener. People want to be heard; but more than that, they want to be listened to.

Action Steps:

1. Pay attention in your conversations with other people and purposely assess yourself after that conversation on a 1–10 scale, with 1 being a really bad listener, and 10 being a really great listener.

2. Do some self-assessment using the same 1–10 scale:
   A. Did I speak over them?
   B. Did I try to top their story?
   C. Did my body language tell them I was listening and interested?
   D. Did I ask pertinent questions that kept the conversation moving?
   E. Did I nod my head and use other gestures and facial expressions to show my interest?
   F. When I had something to contribute, did I interrupt the speaker?
   G. Was I thinking of something to say while I was listening to the speaker?
   H. Did I sit and listen with my arms or legs crossed?
   I. Did I interrupt the speaker when I disagreed with a statement?
   J. Do I make eye contact with people I am speaking with?
   K. Do I pay attention to the body language of the person I am speaking with?
   L. Do I offer encouraging verbal cues when conversing?
   M. How would you rate your overall listening skills?;

Recommended Resources:
Power Listening: Mastering the Most Critical Business Skill of All, by Bernard Ferrari; www.bernieferrari.com
Attitude Pump 176—Treat People Like Today Was Their Birthday, by John Terhune; www.johnterhune.com/attitude

CHAPTER 6

THE ART OF CONVERSATION

The real art of conversation is not only to say the right thing at the right place but to leave unsaid the wrong thing at the tempting moment.—Dorothy Nevill

In our modern world of hashtags and texts with shortcut phrases like OMG (oh my god), LOL (laugh out loud), and SYL (see you later), to name a few, the person who has the ability to have a real, meaningful conversation with a real person will stand out from the crowd in any setting. True conversation is an art form, but one that exhibits enhanced people skills is an elevated art form that will separate you from the masses of people who choose not to discipline themselves in this area of human interaction.

Orchestrated properly by a person with enhanced people skills, a conversation is a beautiful and fulfilling verbal dance. When expert dancers waltz, it is poetic in motion and rhythm—two people become one on the dance floor. That is exactly what should happen in a great conversation: two people talking become one rhythmic, flowing conversation. A key to developing enhanced people skills is to set goals for your conversations, then transition those goals into a regular habit, eventually reaching the point where you no longer think about them. After all, repetition is the mother of mastery. When you get there with practice you will see your life transform in many areas. My personal goals for every conversation are listed below, and as you read through them, you will see that each is simply a manifestation of a person whose ego is in check and who has enough self-esteem that he or she doesn't need to win or even shine in any conversation. I encourage you to intentionally apply these goals to your conversations, see how you do, and determine areas needing improvement.

I want the person with whom I am conversing to feel better about themselves when we are finished conversing than before we began.

Apply this rule in your life, and not only will you be shocked by the number of friends you have, but you will also be blown away by the loyalty you receive from them. Remember my statement early on, that my goal each day is to separate my behavior from that of the masses, assuring me different and better results? The masses are not focused on helping others feel better about themselves—they are concerned with themselves first, and this is apparent during conversations. If you truly care about another person, you realize that you can play a role in helping them develop and maintain their self-image. It is one of the great gifts that one person can give to another: the gift of making that person feel good. The opportunity to give that gift exists in every conversation, and is easily accomplished with words of encouragement and appreciation, and with genuine compliments. Examples:

"Jane, I really respect your opinion on this matter."

"Bill, I just love talking to you about your team because your team pride just flows."

I want that person to feel like the most important person in the conversation.
When you begin a conversation with the specific intent to make the other person the most important person, then your intent will manifest itself in your actions. If your conversation partner feels as though he is the most important person in the conversation, he will be far more willing to open up, warm up, and engage. The more he engages, the more he will enjoy the conversation, and the more he is going to think that you are the world's greatest conversationalist. However, making the other person feel like the most important person in the conversation is not just about listening; it is about you engaging with him. If you are genuinely interested in what he has to say, you will do more than listen—you will ask intelligent, relevant questions; and laugh, smile, and nod at appropriate times. You are part of the dance, not just watching it.

I want that person to be heard.
In my experience, this part of the conversation is a full body experience. For me to convey to my conversation partner that I have heard them, I need to convey that with not only my attentiveness, but my physical responses (e.g., the number of times I smile and nod in agreement). My verbal response should follow the flow of the conversation, and my questions or statements of interest need to be genuine. The flow of the conversation should be a joint endeavor between you and your conversation partner. One easy technique to let people know they are being heard is to repeat what they say in a way that also compliments them. "Jane, I love what you just said. It makes so much sense. I just love the way you think." How could anyone hearing that believe she wasn't being heard or that the person who said it didn't think she was significant and intelligent? Have you ever been in a conversation where it was clear the person with whom you were speaking was not listening; present in body only and not engaged in the conversation? What a terrible insult to dish up to another human being. People want to be heard. To be heard is to be thought of as significant.

I want to use that person's name.

Using someone's name the right number of times is important to the overall feel and flow of any conversation. If you say the person's name in every sentence, you will come off as pandering, but using it at key times in a conversation puts an extra emphasis on your verbal communication. An example might be, "Sue, I couldn't agree more," or "Bill, I love to hear you speak about your children. It is clear to me that you are a remarkable father." If you say the same short sentence without the person's name, you will see that the lack of personalization lessens the impact. Imagine the sound of your name being used as the sound of your favorite tune. This practice is particularly effective if the person you are speaking with is someone you have just met. If you have just been introduced and you mention his or her name in the conversation, it serves the dual purposes of reinforcing that name in your mind and endearing you to your new acquaintance as someone who cares enough to remember his or her name. This skill can be particularly effective in a conversation with several people you have just met, giving you the chance to call each by his or her name during the conversation. I guarantee you will have their attention.

I want to compliment that person in a genuine manner.

Remember that the vast majority of people you speak to might not hear one personal compliment in their average day. I recall a scene from the movie *Clear and Present Danger*, where the CIA deputy chief, played by Harrison Ford, enters his office and, although there is a crisis going on, says to his secretary, "You look very nice today." There was nothing sexual or overt about the compliment, just a genuine "I noticed you" moment that made her day. Most people are so consumed with their own day, they rarely think about the fact that the person they are speaking to may be on the edge of crisis, having a bad day, or deeply concerned with some facet of their life. Everyone experiences a crisis now and again—a genuine compliment can turn a person's day around by providing the one smile needed to make it through the day. My favorite compliment is "That color is you...perfect color choice, you look great." It is a non-threatening compliment that doesn't open the door to misinterpretation. You would be amazed what that simple compliment will evoke in response. Work hard at finding ways to compliment people during conversations. Any chance to make another human being feel good about himself is an opportunity for you to enhance your effectiveness in a conversation. The best practice is to be conservative in this area; if you give too many compliments people will view you as disingenuous.

I want that person to enjoy the conversation and desire further conversations with me.

Can you imagine ending a conversation and getting a hug from the person with whom you were conversing, along with hearing that she really enjoyed talking to you? I can tell you that if that happens, you just received one of the greatest compliments ever. There is no way you would get that response if you had monopolized the conversation, talked more than you listened, were distracted by your cell phone, were in her personal zone, or blowing her hair back with bad breath and interrupting her. You get that response when your verbal and nonverbal actions showed that you value that person, she is important to you, and her feelings and circumstances are significant to you. If you convey those things, you'll need to prepare yourself for a lot of hugs, and sometimes tears. That shows how many people are in need of a genuine conversation with another human being who thinks they are important and special.

I want to use respectful language and tone.

To me, using dirty language or curse words is the sign of a poor vocabulary and a lack of respect. Have you ever watched a movie and not enjoyed it because of the many uses of the *F* word? Whether speaking to a large audience or having a one-on-one conversation, I avoid even mild curse words. Why risk offending someone? Why burn your credibility with this person? I know several people who are described by their friends and acquaintances as having a "trash mouth." Just the other day,

I was talking to a person who referenced a mutual friend by saying that although she was funny, she had a terrible trash mouth. In my world, not only are people unimpressed, they are repulsed by the use of such language. The reason is simple: they can't trust the person not to unleash their trash mouth at an inappropriate time. Using harsh language in conversation will not enhance your people skills; it will diminish them.

I pay particular attention to my tone when I am passionate about something; I have a tendency to go into strong and forceful prosecutor mode. Someone can say the exact same words and sound different to the listener because of tone and inflection. When in doubt, genuine passion and kindness tend to rule the day; it's hard to go wrong when you are speaking from the heart.

I would prefer for them to speak 70 percent of the time and I would prefer to speak 30 percent of the time.

If you want someone to truly enjoy a conversation with you, let them be the star by letting them do about 70 percent of the talking. Remember, if you are talking, you aren't listening, and listening is the greatest skill within your quiver of skills when it comes to having an effective conversation. This balance is best accomplished by combining engaged listening with pertinent questions and commentary that drive the conversation, even though the other person is doing most of the talking. By engaging in the conversation this way, you are acting like an orchestra director. You are directing the flow of the music (conversation), and the musicians are doing the work making the music (conversation). If the orchestra director was not fully engaged in listening, there is no way he could effectively direct. The key here is being fully engaged and responding to the flow of the conversation through questions and comments.

I want my 30 percent of the conversation to be pertinent.

One of the greatest subtle compliments you can give to your conversation partner is to keep what you say highly pertinent and relative. This courtesy shows that you are interested and listening. Have you ever been in a conversation about a subject important to you, and your conversation partner began to talk about a totally different subject? Or maybe gave a response out of the flow of the conversation and highly irrelevant? If you have experienced that, then you know your partner might as well have told you he was bored with what you were talking about and has decided to move on to another subject. A conversation partner with the right intent is focused on what the other person is saying and how she is saying it. It comes back to the issue of who is the most important person in the conversation? Is it you or the other person? If you were talking with the President, the Pope, or a favorite sports star, would your responses and conversation be highly pertinent and focused, based on what the other person was saying? Of course they would.

I want my body language to show I am highly interested.

Years as a trial lawyer dramatically sharpened my skills specific to body language and its effect on people. To me, body language speaks much louder than words, and I could always tell by watching body language when jurors did not believe a witness. They couldn't say out it loud, but with my trained eye, they didn't need to say it out loud. When I read disbelief of a witness in jurors' body language, I would then direct my closing argument to those who "told" me they didn't believe that witness. I knew if I argued in closing that the witness was not to be believed, if I paid particular attention with my eye contact and direction of my argument to those jurors, that I would be enhancing my case with them.

Body language has become almost a musical instrument for me during a conversation. When I speak with someone, I don't just sit or stand there. My body language speaks as clearly as the words from my mouth. Whether it is a nod of agreement, a surprised look, a change in posture, a smile, a laugh, an inquisitive look, a gasp, a dropping of the jaw, a shaking of the head or a simple leaning forward, my partners in a conversation can clearly see I am listening. If you ever have a chance to observe someone with enhanced people skills engaged in a conversation, you will see that their body is in the flow of the conversation throughout.

I want to share my story, not top theirs.

I have been blessed with an amazing life that has included traveling to more than thirty countries, and making thousands of friends from all walks of life all over the world. Having considered life an adventure, I have experienced many things that most people can only read about in books. This area is a challenge to me that I am constantly working on to improve. It is rare when I am talking to someone about a trip to a particular country where I can't top their story of their experience with those of my own. This recently happened in speaking to someone about a trip to Italy. My story of my experience was simply extraordinary compared to their rather modest experiences of that country. But instead of topping their story I mentioned that my wife and I had recently visited also. That gave me the ability to ask great pertinent questions about their trip. My questions to them drove the conversation. So what was your favorite part of the country? What was your favorite meal? Where did you stay? If I were to go back next year what would you advise me about that city? Would you recommend that restaurant when I return? Do you think that was a great time of year to be there or would you choose another time of year? When you return what would you spend more time doing? What would you spend less time doing? The focus of the conversation was about their experience, not mine.

I want to smile and make eye contact.

By not looking at the jury while testifying, a witness damages their credibility. I coached my witnesses to look at the jury, and would position myself at the far end of the jury box to make it more natural to look at the jury during their testimony. If I was questioning the defendant or one of their witnesses, I positioned myself away from the jury box, so that the witness was looking away from the jury during questioning. Human beings use eye contact as a means of discerning truth and sincerity.

It has been said that the eyes are the window to the soul. The eyes are the most effective means of communicating truth, emotion, compassion, and empathy. There is a huge difference between great eye contact during a conversation and simply staring during a conversation. It drives me crazy to be in a conversation with someone who spends most of the time looking away or down. That is an outward manifestation of a poor self-image, a lack of confidence, or both.

I want an ease to the conversation like a rhythmic dance.

If you observe a great conversationalist, even if you are unable to hear the words, you see a flow happening. You see constantly changing body actions in response to what is being said. You would see timely smiles and laughter. You would see nodding, shaking of the head and a clear give and take between the participants in the conversation. But most importantly you would observe an ease—actions and body language that say she is enjoying this conversation.

I want to say "you," not "I" during the conversation.

The next time you have a conversation or overhear a conversation between two people, pay attention to how many times you hear the word *I*. If you use *I* too much, that is a loud signal that this conversation is about you, not them; if you use *you* more often, the conversation is about them. That is not to say *I* shouldn't be used at all; just use it minimally. Apply the 70/30 rule of listening versus talking to your use of *I* versus *you*.

I want to show that I am well read and able to discuss many subjects.

You will dramatically enhance your potential as a great conversationalist by being well read and informed on current issues. I am a voracious reader, and there are few occasions where I cannot make intelligent conversation on a subject. Whether it's financial, sports, business, politics, trends, or history, rare is the moment where I can't delve into any subject that arises. That arsenal of insight comes from a purposed habit of staying informed. Becoming well read doesn't take years of study—it takes staying plugged in to the happenings of the world. In today's world of instant information, that is very easy to do. Just a little extra effort in this area can make you deep in many areas. Here are some suggestions:

➤ Have a favorite author

➤ Follow a favorite sports team

➤ Follow financial trends through investment newsletters

➤ Follow political activities and hot topics

➤ Choose a reliable news source and invest a few minutes each day to keep up

➤ Stay current on movies

➤ Sample the dining-out options of your area

➤ Participate in events that excite you

➤ Work on being interesting through the things you are interested in

I want to inject light, tasteful humor into the conversation.

People enjoy things more when they are smiling or laughing. Any time I do a training or presentation, I know that the audience will recall more if they are laughing on the way to learning. Humor engages another aspect of the human being. It causes people to lower their defenses and engage more as a participant in the conversation. I don't need to make the person roll on the floor laughing, but if I can invoke my wit to make them smile, that changes the dynamics of the conversation.

I want to maintain appropriate personal space between me and my conversation partner.

Remember the "close talker" from *Seinfeld*? That character got right up in the face of the person he was speaking to, making them very uncomfortable. When someone is in my personal zone, I am simply not listening; I am counting down the seconds before he gets out of my face. Have you ever had this experience? There is a proper distance that you should keep from people when speaking, and getting in someone's personal zone will turn most people off very quickly. He won't hear you; he will be too busy praying the conversation will end soon.

I want the person to know I was not distracted during our conversation.

On a recent trip to Rome, I took a picture of four people sitting at an outside café. Every one of them was looking at a phone screen, obviously communicating with someone not at the table. Have you ever been speaking to someone who began typing a message on their phone or checking e-mail? How did you feel? You certainly didn't feel you were a priority for this person. When I have a conversation, I want all of me engaged in that conversation. It is the only way to have my conversation partner be the center of my attention.

I want my breath to be pleasant and not invasive.

Many people don't realize that their effectiveness in a conversation is completely obliterated by bad breath. Now, this may sound ridiculous, yet I know you have experienced someone with nuclear bad breath speaking to you. Who is going to listen or engage in a protracted conversation under these circumstances? Remember, the conversation should be a verbal waltz. Would you like to waltz with someone whose bad breath bent your eyeglass frames? Having traveled the world for business, I am truly amazed what a significant problem this is in business settings. If it is a problem in business settings, one must assume it is every bit that much of a problem in everyday conversations. I knew a gentleman who simply could not succeed in sales until someone (me) cared enough to tell him the truth about his terrible bad breath.

I do not want to interrupt or talk over my conversation partner.

When I observe people in conversation, this is the area where I see most people fall down. Most either interrupt or talk over the other person during conversations. This means they are not listening, and are not making the other person the star of the conversation. Interrupting means they have been formulating a response while the person talked, and could not have been totally listening. They simply can't keep it in, and have to release their response. As I mentioned in chapter 4, when I watch news shows and two guests are debating an issue, I hate to hear them speak over each other—I am much more likely to listen to the person who respectfully listens, despite their disagreement, and responds in a respectful manner.

I want to recognize the person's personality type and tailor the conversation to suit that type.

In my considerable study of the human species during sixty years of living life, I am convinced that people are wired very differently. Now you may be thinking facetiously, "Terhune, you are a genius." Before you get too far down this road, allow me to make a point that will dramatically sharpen your conversation skills: different personalities respond to different styles of conversation. For instance, there are people who are very serious by nature. They have to work up to a smile or a grin let alone a laugh. They are about facts and logic. There are others who are very sanguine in nature. They are about having fun, laughing, and having a great time in all aspects of life. If you try to talk to these very different personalities the same way, you will not be as effective as you could be. I want to tailor my conversation style to best fit the personality of the person with whom I am speaking so that she is in her comfort zone. The more comfortable someone is with you, the more likely she is to open up, have a great conversation, and enjoy the experience.

I don't want to formulate my response while someone else is speaking.

Some of you may realize this is a significant issue for you. When someone else is making a point, you are thinking about your response. Physiologically, you cannot be completely listening to someone if this dynamic is going on in your head. The good news is that this is a practice that you can modify quickly. It really boils down to what the mission of your conversation is in the first place. If your mission is anything short of making the other person feel heard, appreciated, and respected, it is easy to default to the "formulate your answer in your head while he is talking" mode. Conversely, if your mission is to make the other participant feel heard, appreciated, and respected, you will listen intently to everything he says using your ears as well as your body language. Believe me, your brain is fast enough to come up with a great response after the person has stopped talking and you are finished listening effectively.

The key to becoming a conversation artist is being cognizant of these goals. As you think about them over time, they become a natural consequence of any conversation that you have. Remember, repetition is the mother of mastery.

Action Steps:

1. Be aware of your mission in conversing with other people; make them the focus, not you.
2. Be fully engaged by listening with your ears and your entire person.
3. Set a daily goal to make others feel better about themselves having conversed with you.

Recommended Resources:

Skill with People, by Les Giblin; www.skillwithpeople.com

Attitude Pump 161—The Attitude of Humility, by John Terhune; www.john-terhune.com/attitude

CHAPTER 7

THE POWER OF YOUR SMILE

The expression one wears on one's face is far more important than the clothes one wears on one's back.—Dale Carnegie

If you genuinely smile, it is almost impossible to have anything but a great attitude. Start your day with a regimen of smiles. It creates an inner expectation that your day is going to be great. One of the greatest people skill secrets is to smile at people during conversations. It projects you as a friendly, warm, happy person, and makes a huge difference in how people interact with you. If you will make a habit of having smiling "fits" during your day, I assure you it will affect your interactions with other people. You will find people more welcoming. You will find them warmer and more willing to engage in conversation. You will actually find them smiling back becasue smiling is a natural response to someone smiling at you.

In my early professional life as a trial lawyer, I was not a person who wore a smile during much of the day. If you knew me way back then, you would have described me as intense. I was focused and my face showed it. I clearly had not learned about the power inherent in smiling at another human being. Now, as simple as this may seem, most people do not understand how a smile can change a day for another person. A smile can be a transformational moment in another person's day.

A lady in my spinning class at the YMCA has one of the greatest smiles I have ever seen. When she walks in, she lights up the room with her positive aura and genuine smile. Her smile is telling the world she is a happy person, her life is great, and that nothing is going to steal her great attitude. By the way, her smile is contagious—it is impossible not to smile back at her and feel the connection to the happy person she represents through her smile.

Les Giblin, in his book *Skills with People* said, "if you are not using your smile, you are like a man with a million dollars in the bank and no checkbook." Have you ever noticed the contestants in a beauty pageant? When they come on stage, the first thing you notice are their smiles. Have you ever noticed how often a politician is smiling on her campaign materials? Politicians are in the business of people skills—if you think about the most successful politicians of our time, you can see the smile they bring to their life and public persona. President Obama has great people skills, but among his greatest assets is his smile.

Have you ever been on a flight and noticed the different moods of the flight attendants? When you come across one who is smiling, you feel welcomed on the plane. The same person could be without a smile and you would have a completely different feel from them.

Imagine you are interviewing two closely qualified job candidates. One wears a frown, the other wears a warm smile. Does that smile or frown set the tone for the interview? Try standing in front of the mirror wearing a neutral facial expression, then put a great big smile on your face. Who you would you rather deal with? I know people who are average looking but become striking when smiling because of the positive energy that is emoted from their smile. If you desire to become more attractive, smile more. A smile can lift another's heart. When my wife, children, or grandchildren smile at me there are few moments more special in my life.

A smile truly has the power to change someone's day or life. Have you ever been having a terrible day, but someone presents you with a huge smile? A genuine smile has transformational powers. You can settle someone's fear, insecurity, hurt, or anxiety with something as simple as a smile. The next time someone you know is feeling sad, scared, or nervous, try smiling with them.

There is even a famous rap song called the "Power of a Smile" that contains the following lyrics:

> *The power of a gun can kill, and the power of fire can burn; the power of wind can chill, and the power of mind can learn; the power of anger, can raise inside until it tears you apart but the power of a smile, especially yours, can heal a frozen heart.*

When you're smiling, no doubt you're having a much better time than when you're not smiling—it simply makes you feel better! Research has shown that smiling releases serotonin, a neurotransmitter that produces feelings of happiness and wellbeing. It's like a circle of happiness—smile and you feel happy; feel happy and you smile! Even when you're not feeling great, try smiling. Note the difference you feel. The only thing more powerful than one person smiling is two people smiling at each other.

OK. I think you get the inherent power of a smile. Now, how can we leverage that knowledge into a more effective you? Business deals can be made simply through smiling. One of the first things that salespeople learn is to smile. Would you rather buy something from the bored sales rep or the smiling sales rep? A smiling person would be much more enthusiastic about the product and instill positive feelings in the buyer. Even phone salespeople and customer service reps are taught to smile while they speak to a customer—cadence and tone are very different when you are smiling than when you are not, and customers can hear the difference.

If you are in business, think of how many new people you meet, how many first impressions you make each day. Smiling is crucial when it comes to first impressions, and when you meet someone, it will indicate you are genuinely happy to see them and that you are a positive person. Smiling invites conversation and lowers the guard of the person you present with your smile.

Smiling can be a powerful form of body language that tells the other person you are engaged in what she is saying. Small smiles can be used to demonstrate that the listener is paying attention, or as a way of agreeing or being happy about the messages being received. Combined with nods of the head, smiles can be powerful in affirming that messages are being listened to and understood.

One way to become better at smiling is by increasing your awareness. Take notice of those you find warm and inviting. Is it because of their smile? Make an effort to look for great smiles. Notice the appeal of people who smile with their eyes, not just their mouth. The whole face gets involved. Study yourself in the mirror. Do you look more friendly and approachable when smiling? Did you know that you use fewer muscles smiling than you do frowning? There is only one person who has control over the face that you bring to life—you. Smiling is a choice. It is an outward manifestation of the inner person. It tells people who you are inside at the moment and welcomes them to engage with you as a fellow human being. People want to engage with happy people. A smile tells the world there is happiness within you.

Action Steps:

1. Stand in front of a mirror and note the vast difference between the smiling you and the nonsmiling you.

2. Practice smiling while you are on the phone with someone and note the difference in your tone and attitude toward them.

3. Enter every room with a smile.

Recommended Resources:

Smile: The Astonishing Power of a Simple Act (TED Books), by Ron Gutman; www.ted.com/talks/ron_gutman_the_hidden_power_of_smiling

Attitude Pump 125—The Power of a Smile, by John Terhune; www.johnterhune. com/attitude

CHAPTER 8

THE POWER OF A GREAT AND POLITE SENSE OF HUMOR

Anybody with a good sense of humor is one up on the competition. We respond to someone who has the ability to make us laugh. It is a bonding influence.—Anonymous

One reason I have been intrigued with politics all of my life is that to become an elected official, particularly on a national level like president, you simply must be likeable and have extraordinary people skills. The first president I have clear recollection of (I was born in 1953) is President John F. Kennedy. Since my early days in college, I have followed political races and personalities within those races. It is simply fascinating to me. Actually, a brief focus on several presidents will illustrate several points about the importance of a good sense of humor.

The first president with a reputation for a quick wit and great sense of humor was Abraham Lincoln. This has always intrigued me about

Lincoln, and many theorize that his humor allowed him to weather the tortuous days of the Civil War.

The term "sense of humor" wasn't in common usage until about the time of the Civil War. In the 1840s and 1850s, people had a "sense of the ridiculous." As you would expect, that term didn't have the positive connotations that "sense of humor" has today.

Lincoln's humor stood out because it was more like humor as we know it today. We don't make the distinction between wit and humor anymore, but in the nineteenth century people did. Wit was sarcastic and antipathetic; humor was congenial and empathetic. It's the difference between and "laughing at" or "laughing with" someone, and Lincoln was much more about "laughing with," though he often used self-effacing humor to laugh at himself. In the famous Lincoln-Douglas debates, Stephen Douglas accused Lincoln of being two-faced, to which Lincoln replied, referencing his appearance, "Honestly, if I were two-faced, would I be showing you this one?"

You can see his humor in many sayings attributed to President Lincoln:

> ➤ *Tact: the ability to describe others as they see themselves.*

> ➤ *Better to remain silent and be thought a fool than to speak out and remove all doubt.*

> ➤ *He can compress the most words into the smallest ideas better than any man I ever met.*

> ➤ *No matter how much cats fight, there always seems to be plenty of kittens.*

> ➤ *I'm a success today because I had a friend who believed in me and I didn't have the heart to let him down.*

> *After forty, every man gets the face he deserves.*

> *I am a firm believer in the people. If given the truth, they can be depended upon to meet any national crisis. The great point is to bring them the real facts, and beer.*

> *Whenever I hear anyone arguing for slavery, I feel a strong impulse to see it tried on him personally.*

Clearly, Lincoln used his humor as a tool of endearment to his audiences and to effectively illustrate a point or win a debate among his political peers and adversaries.

A century later, a young, vibrant John F. Kennedy took the stage as the president of our country. His humorous banter with the press became his trademark. His ease and self-confidence found a natural expression through his humor. An important point about Kennedy's humor is that it was light, many times self-effacing, and delivered in a relaxed fashion with a great smile or a boyish grin. The lesson there is that his humor was natural and easy; it was part of his nature.

Forced humor never comes off well. Whether you are addressing a group or speaking with someone one-on-one, fun humor is always better than cutting humor. Kennedy used fun humor that was consequential to his overall persona; a natural reflection of what was on the inside and how he processed the events of his world. When you deliver humor in that way (with ease as a natural flow from the way you approach life) you are telling the world you don't take anything too seriously. It says you see the funny side of the human experience and enjoy that aspect of your life. When people sense that quality from you they find you pleasant to be around.

During Kennedy's 1960 presidential campaign. pundits and opponents complained that he came from huge money. To that he replied simply, "I just received the following wire from my generous Daddy: Dear

Jack, Don't buy a single vote more than is necessary. I'll be damned if I am going to pay for a landslide."

When he appointed his brother Bobby as attorney general despite cries of nepotism, he responded with "I see nothing wrong with giving Robert some legal experience as attorney general before he goes out to practice law."

When a young boy asked him how he became a war hero, he gracefully responded that "it was absolutely involuntary; they sunk my boat."

Kennedy's ability to be warm and self-effacing generated approval that has only increased with time. He brilliantly utilized this great sense of humor to disarm even the most negative of critics. Humor used correctly is one of the very best tools to enhance your people skills. This doesn't mean you need to memorize jokes; you simply need to recognize and appreciate the funny side of life and not take things too seriously. Actually, the funniest person in your life is probably you, if you could simply see the funny aspects of you going through life.

Two decades later, President Ronald Reagan became known as the great communicator—he could deliver a message that would inspire confidence and optimism perhaps better than any politician in our history, yet his sense of humor is every bit a part of his legacy as his keen ability to make one proud to be an American. Actually, a beautifully timed line by Reagan turned the lights out on Walter Mondale during the 1984 presidential race. Reagan and Mondale were squared off in a debate watched closely by the nation. Reagan's age (he was into his seventies) was brought up by the debate commentator, and Mondale argued that age did matter; that Reagan's advanced age should be considered. Reagan responded, "I want you to know that I will not make age an issue of this campaign. I am not going to exploit, for political purposes, my opponent's youth and inexperience." This drew thunderous laughter and it took five minutes to quiet the crowd. Even Mondale couldn't help breaking into a visible and genuine state of laughter.

Even immediately after President Reagan had been shot and he was being taken into surgery, his sense of humor simply couldn't be contained as he told surgeons: "I hope you are all Republicans." In his tenure as president, he had many famous lines of humor:

> *Thomas Jefferson once said, "We should never judge a president by his age, only by his works." And ever since he told me that, I stopped worrying.—on critics of his age.*
>
> *There is absolutely no circumstance whatever under which I would accept that spot. Even if they tied and gagged me, I would find a way to signal by wiggling my ears.—on possibly being offered the vice presidency in 1968.*
>
> *Politics is not a bad profession. If you succeed, there are many rewards. If you disgrace yourself, you can always write a book.*

Each of these presidents had extraordinary people skills. They could not have reached the heights of their brilliant careers with anything less. Many times their humor was self-effacing, and through their example we clearly see how making someone laugh connects and endears us to each other. It accelerates the "like" factor. It makes your ability to communicate a point or point of view far more effective. Mark Twain said that humor was mankind's greatest blessing. William Thackeray said that good humor is one of the best articles of dress one can wear in society. I say that humor, delivered in good taste at the right time can dramatically enhance your level of people skills.

Action Steps:

1. Lighten up and watch for the funny side of the life you are living.
2. Realize that you and your life are the source of great humor.

Recommended Resources:

Lincoln Tells a Joke. How Laughter Saved the President (and the Country), by Kathleen Krull; www.goodreads.com/book/show/6826049-lincoln-tells-a-joke

Attitude Pump 114—Happy in Today, by John Terhune; www.johnterhune. com/attitude

CHAPTER 9

DEALING WITH NEGATIVE AND DIFFICULT PEOPLE

I am thankful for all the negative people in my life; they have shown me who I do not want to be.—Anonymous

Working for ten years as a trial lawyer, I have had a life full of experience in dealing with negative and difficult people; you might even call me an expert in this area. This is one of the most important aspects of developing enhanced people skills because, like it or not, you will always have to deal with negative and difficult people. They are all around us. The good news is that if you can learn to deal with negative or difficult people, then you can deal with anyone.

Dealing with difficult or negative people is a game I enjoy. I view these exchanges as challenges to my skill set. These people are the ones who demand the best of me when it comes to people skills. When something great happens as the result of dealing with people like this, the victory seems a bit sweeter; the climb to success was steeper.

As we begin this chapter let's get an understanding of negative people and distinguish them from difficult people. Negative people have a pessimistic and limited view of the world, based on their negative attitude. You know people like this: For them, if the day is warm, then it is too hot. If the day is cool, it is too cold. If it is sunny, it is too bright. They have a difficult time finding the positive in anything. The glass is half empty not half full. They view life through the lens of negativity. After working with thousands of people in many different countries, I have come to conclude some people simply enjoy being negative. *Saturday Night Live* featured the character Debbie Downer in many of their skits. She would usually appear at social gatherings and interrupt the conversation to voice negative opinions and pronouncements. My guess is that you have "Debbie Downers" in your life. If they don't have something to complain about then they are not happy. Their personal misery through their negative lens is a comforting place for them. It empowers them to make sense of their world. For most people in this category you are not going to change them however; you can learn to communicate with them in an effective and even encouraging manner. I have seen people who are negative destroy teams, morale, levels of expectation, and confidence in management. If a negative person is seeking to cause damage, he can quickly prove that the power of negative is every bit as compelling as the power of positive.

Difficult people use their contentious nature to gain the advantage. When I say "a difficult person," I am talking about someone who is negative and caustic in their approach to everything. Difficult people typically seek to gain advantage through that difficult nature. I remember talking to a fellow lawyer at a bar association luncheon in the town where we practiced. He had a reputation as a complete and total jerk. As I chatted with him, I asked where he had gone to law school and what it was that brought him to this town to practice law. He was surprisingly personable, unlike the character that so vigorously represented his clients. He told me that when he was searching for a town to practice law, he quickly realized that this one didn't have an A**hole Attorney to represent people in divorces—he decided to practice here to fill the void. I congratulated him on being so successful in fulfilling his mission. What he was really saying to me was that he knew difficult people often get their way because others simply do not know how to deal with them.

So let's analyze difficult people so that we have a better understanding of why they are as they are. Then let's create an effective strategy to deal with them.

My attorney friend aside, let's assume it is the minority of difficult people who actually set out to be difficult. If you could "peel the onion," you would find that most of them act this way because of a poor self-image or an emotional hurt left unhealed. Their difficult nature is simply a reflection of what is going on inside of them. If you keep this in mind, it changes the way you handle them. Below are a series of strategies that I utilize when dealing with negative and difficult people.

Pick your battles. One of the greatest lessons that I learned in the courtroom was choosing when to fight. I knew lawyers who would object to every question asked, and fight over every minor legal point while trying a case. It didn't take long to see that this wore out the judge, and over the course of a longer trial, frustrated the jurors. I took a very different approach: I objected to and fought only issues that would make a difference. The judges of my circuit came to know this, often ruling in my favor; they knew I wasn't fighting over the little stuff, just the important stuff.

The same rule should be applied to dealing with negative or difficult people—pick your battles. Resist the urge to fight if it is not an issue that will make a substantial difference to an important matter. If it is not a point where the outcome makes a difference, there is no need to engage with what is most likely an irrational position.

Be a grown-up. Children *react*, but a confident, thoughtful adult *responds*. When someone is particularly negative or difficult, their thoughts pour from their mouth with very little discretion, much like a cranky toddler. The adult in the room contemplates what has been said and responds in a calm and collected manner. If you want to drive a negative or difficult person crazy, don't stoop to their level. Their level is typically emotional, but you can maintain the upper hand by staying safely in the land of the rational and thoughtful.

Focus on problem solving. Negative and difficult people typically focus on the problem, not the solution. Focusing on the problem gives them cause in their mind to live in the land of negative. It justifies their position. The more you agree with them and get negative with them, the more you fuel their negativity. The more you give them attention and listen with a calm, adult manner, the more you will turn the conversation into a discussion of solutions:

> *Jim, it is clear to me that you are very unhappy about this issue. I hear you and I totally understand where you are coming from. Would you mind terribly conspiring with me to come up with some solutions so we can get your heart back in the game?*

When focusing on solutions, it never hurts to "pour on a little honey." Gentle compliments can serve to ease the vinegar of negativity. You should state your position openly and clearly—a person with enhanced people skills should be able to soften their aggression through respectful and complimentary words:

> *Jim, I love your passion. As your friend and cheerleader, I want to help you channel it to finding a solution that works for you and everyone else.*

They can't get your goat if they don't know where it is tied (Responding versus Reacting). If you react emotionally to something that a negative or difficult person does, instead of responding rationally, you just let them know "where your goat is tied." This is a Southern colloquialism that is powerful in its truth. When you reveal to another what it is that sets you off, you have relinquished control to that person. Now he knows how to "get your goat" or "get under your skin." Negative and difficult people tend to prey on those in whom they can provoke an emotional response. Refuse to be that person: practice reflection and a slow response, as opposed to an emotional and quick response.

Being a great listener is the best offense. There is no need to play defense against negative or difficult people when playing offense is so easy. If you view a negative person as a bag of wind that will eventually run out of air, then you realize being a good listener is the best offense with these types of people. Keep in mind there are times when all these people want is to be heard. Let them purge. View your listening as a purge valve in their life and then turn the conversation to a solution-oriented conversation instead of a negative dumping ground focused only on the problem. Keep your questions constructive and probing. This is not to say that you should acquiesce to every issue—it is critical that you champion your perspective and solutions. The key is in how you do this. In every situation dealing with a negative or difficult person, there are two factors present: your relationship with this person, and the issue you are discussing. A person with enhanced people skills knows how to separate the person from the issue, and be soft on the person yet firm on the issue:

> *Jim, I want to talk about what's bothering you, but I can't do it when you are in this state and unwilling to have a conversation that will lead to solutions. Let's either sit down and have a civil discussion, or take a time out and come back this afternoon.*

Make sure your posture disguises what you may be feeling at the moment. Remember that your body language speaks as loud as or louder than the words from your mouth. If a negative or difficult person is making you angry or intimidating you, it is very important to keep your body language from revealing this. You have to have your body language as well as your verbal language respond to the circumstances instead of react to the circumstances. For instance, crossing your arms in reaction to the negative person is showing a defensive you and creating a communication barrier. It is also telling that person that they are getting to you. Remember, you are the adult in the room. Don't take it personally even if it sounds personal. It is the weaker person who tries to gain the advantage through negative words and actions.

Action Steps:
1. Always be the grown-up in the room.
2. Don't let them know where your goat is tied.
3. Redirect the conversation to be solution focused instead of problem focused.

Recommended Resources:
Adversaries into Allies, by Bob Burg; www.burg.com/books/

Attitude Pump 130—Be a Solution-Oriented Thinker, by John Terhune; www.johnterhune.com/attitude

CHAPTER 10

THE AMAZING POWER OF REMEMBERING SOMEONE'S NAME

A person's name is to that person the sweetest and most important sound in any language.—Dale Carnegie

Have you ever been introduced to someone, but couldn't remember their name by the end of the brief conversation? This chapter covers a subject I take particular pride in, in my personal and professional life. Perhaps it was my early training as a trial lawyer, when I memorized the names of prospective jurors during *voir dire* (to tell the truth) that made me realize the importance of remembering people's names. Perhaps it has been the thousands of people I have met in business settings over the last twenty-five years that brought the importance of remembering names to the forefront of my mind when it comes to people skills. Then again, it probably was a combination of all of my experiences with people over the years.

Whatever the reason, if you ever meet someone who knows me, you will hear that I am remarkable at remembering people's names. I am certainly not perfect, but I am good enough for people to mention time and again how amazing they think I am in this area. Imagine how you would feel if we had met for a business luncheon more than a year ago, but we cross paths in an airport and I remember your name. Would you feel special? Would you feel as though you must be someone special to be remembered after a year? Would you remember that I remembered your name and maybe even mention it to other people? That happens to me all the time. Why? Because I decided to make remembering names a priority. This is something I work at constantly. I make it a priority because I know it makes people feel special. We have all heard that people don't care what you know until they know that you care. However trite that may sound, it is absolutely true. There are few things more impactful than remembering their name, to show the person you are talking to is important.

The brilliant and groundbreaking author on people skills, Dale Carnegie, is quoted as saying:

Increase your desire to remember names by constantly reminding yourself how the ability to remember names will:

1. *Enhance your popularity.*
2. *Help you in your business or profession.*
3. *Help you win friends.*
4. *Give sparkle to your social contacts.*
5. *Help you practice the Golden Rule by "doing unto others..."*
6. *Prevent embarrassment by showing you are genuinely interested in others.*

To further the point, Carnegie considered this skill so critical that he included it with his principles on human relations:

Principle Six: Remember that a person's name, to that person, is the sweetest, most important sound in any language.

I can tell you that this skill set can be enhanced by you by deciding to improve in this vital area of people skills. If you invest the time to get good in this area, it will pay huge dividends in your personal and business life and will go a long way toward people describing you as having outstanding people skills.

This skill set boils down to three things:

1. Making the decision to enhance your skill set specific to remembering people's names.

2. Being patient with yourself in the development of this skill as you improve with time and practice. Getting great in this area is a process, not an event.

3. Develop a personal methodology that works for you. There is no magic formula here. The key is to keep it simple and repeat the methodology enough that it becomes second nature.

If there were a magical formula to becoming great in this area beyond a consistently focused effort, I would certainly share it with you. But there is no such thing. Remembering names is a skill, not a magical process. And like any other skill, you can develop and strengthen it so that it is ready when you need it.

A different method of sharpening this very important arrow in your quiver of people skills comes down to finding what works for you best. What works for me may not work for you. I tend to approach things pragmatically and don't find that gimmicks work well for me. With that in mind, allow me to set forth some of the habits I have developed that have helped me stand out.

First, when I meet someone for the first time, I find it very helpful to say her name out loud during the introduction. So instead of saying, "It is very nice to meet you," I say, "Mary, it is very nice to meet you." Saying her name out loud imprints it on my brain. As the conversation progresses, I make it a point to say her name several times, thus deepening the imprint of her name and face. Always remember that repetition is the mother of mastery.

Next, I make a mental note connecting the name and face of this new person with someone already imprinted in my brain. Two weeks ago in my exercise class (where I know the name of 90 percent of the daily participants), a woman came in whose name I did not know. I introduced myself to her and she told me her name was Debbie. I immediately said, "Great to meet you, Debbie" (beginning the imprint by saying her name out loud), then mentally connected her face and general appearance to a business associate of mine named Debbie who was similar in stature and hair color (deepening the imprint). She didn't return to class for almost two weeks but came into class today. I know she was taken aback when I said, "Good morning, Debbie," as she entered the class, but I'm sure she was thinking, "This guy is really good with remembering names."

Mentally making a connection to someone or something tangible after saying the name of the person out loud is a powerful reinforcement or "anchoring" for your brain. My anchoring could involve a movie star's name, a character in a movie, or a place. For instance, if someone's name is Georgia, I want to say the name out loud and then see a peach on her head or hear the song "Georgia on My Mind." If someone's name is Wilson, I envision Wilson, Tom Hanks's volleyball in the movie *Cast Away*, on the head of my new acquaintance. And if I am introduced to Caroline, I will say her name out loud, but in my brain I will sing Neil Diamond's "Sweet Caroline." If you practice this powerful anchoring method, you will find yourself increasingly proficient in name memory while having fun along the way. Your brain is an amazing organ that has a memory capability far beyond what you might think. Your job is to imprint the information in such a way that it creates long-term memory or at least easy access to the person's name. Association is a powerful tool to further anchor your brain's recognition of a person's name.

My final but most important method of name memory is also the most basic, least innovative, and most effective, particularly when combined with the previous two habits: I invest the time to write the person's name down on my "Names I Need to Remember" sheet. Now please note that I have purposely used the word *invest* instead of *take*. This simple habit is an investment in the human beings who are entering your life.

Remember, it is all about separating your daily habits from those of the average person. When I meet someone new, their name is going on my sheet. Then, over the next several days, I will view that paper and the name on it, thus reinforcing the memory of the meeting and the introduction. Again, this simple yet powerful method is further anchoring the name in my brain. That list of people stays close to me at my office workstation. It takes a mere few seconds each day to review and refresh it with names of new people I have met. Remember: say the name out loud, associate it with something else, write it down. It's that easy.

Recently, I was in a day-long business meeting with a group of consultants. The first thing I did after being introduced was to write their name on the paper where I'd be taking notes during the day's meeting. I could glance at that list of names in writing, interact with the people during the day, and cement the names in my mind. The brain plus the pen equals a powerful memory enhancer.

I promise you that making the effort to improve in this area will pay you huge dividends in your personal and professional life. All it takes is the desire to improve followed by the disciplined application of a few simple techniques to make enormous strides of success.

Action Steps:

1. Follow my protocol of saying the name, anchoring it, and writing it down.
2. If my protocol doesn't work for you, create one that does.
3. Set a goal to be known as a person who is great at remembering people's names.

Recommended Resources:

Remember Every Name Every Time, by Benjamin Levy; www.benjaminlevymemory.com

Attitude Pump 172—Take Action Now, by John Terhune; www.johnterhune.com/attitude

CHAPTER 11

PUNCTUALITY EQUALS RESPECT

Better three hours too soon, than one minute too late.—William Shakespeare

I have a simple rule when it comes to being on time: if I am always early, I am never late. This has served me very well over my career as trial lawyer and success coach. If you are thinking "What does being on time have to do with people skills?" my answer is that being on time screams to another person either respect or disrespect, and thus has a huge amount to do with how you are viewed by other people. How you are viewed by people ultimately is determined by your degree of people skills and punctuality is a vitally important people skill.

Your integrity is an essential ingredient in being viewed favorably and liked by other people. If you are on time you are telling the people that you respect their time. The most valuable commodity that any human being has is their time. If you are late in meeting people, you are saying your time is more valuable than their time and that you respect your time more than theirs. What a terrible message to send to someone. I would far rather send the message by my timeliness that I respect your time and I keep my word—I am here just as I promised.

I cannot begin to tell you how many times I have sat in a parking lot one minute away from my destination but thirty minutes early, to assure myself that I could find the location and be there on time. I have made this a trademark of my craft as an attorney, consultant, coach and keynote speaker. By being on time, I am keeping my word. If I agree to a time, then I have given my word that I will be there at that time. I never take the chance that all will be well in my journey to a meeting or event. I always assume something is going to happen to slow or disrupt the journey.

Also, I like to be "together" when beginning a meeting—particularly a meeting that has consequences. If I am running late and getting stressed and worried about getting there on time, my character is different than if I have arrived early and gathered my thoughts prior to the meeting. There are many times when a meeting is the first impression someone will have of you. I want my first impression to be one that impresses and demonstrates professionalism and respect; being on time says exactly that. Being in the businesses that I am in, I am very aware of my personal brand. Being on time enhances my brand; being late would tarnish it.

Imagine that you are set to interview for a life-changing new job. This job is what you have been working toward for years. Would you make a point of being on time for the interview? Would you get there thirty minutes to an hour early just to be sure that nothing would go wrong in your journey? Of course you would. The question then becomes, why wouldn't you make being prompt a habit that you apply on every occasion? This again is one of those areas where you can separate yourself from the behavior of the average person. The average person doesn't make being prompt a priority. The average person doesn't show up early to eliminate the possibility of problems in the journey. The average person doesn't treat his word as gold and do what he says he is going to do.

Being prompt, respecting others' time, and keeping your word are vital people skills. If you were to interview people in my life, from family members to professional colleagues, they would tell you that I am always on time. I am so dedicated to being on time, my friends and colleagues would bet a lot of money on my prompt arrival to any event or meeting they host. They know their bet would be safe because they know I am absolutely over-the-moon crazy on this subject. Being on time shows respect for others' time. Being on time says that I keep my word and I do what I say. Being late shows arrogance and a disrespect for the valuable time of others. Being chronically on time is a matter of discipline and making it a priority. It is a decision you should make and follow through with in your professional and personal life.

I know people (no names mentioned to protect the guilty) who are so chronically late that I will tell them a time that is thirty minutes to an hour before the real time knowing they will be thirty minutes to an hour late and thus right on time. I recently hosted a dinner party and one of these offenders, who has been late by at least thirty minutes for years, arrived right on time for this occasion. Of course, little did he know I had given him a time one hour prior to the actual start time.

My craziness on this subject would have to take second place to legendary football coach Vince Lombardi's. Coach Lombardi was known for instilling discipline that supported precise execution. His punctuality philosophy became known as "Lombardi Time."

According to former players, Vince Lombardi had a special version of time—one that ran fifteen minutes earlier than any normal clock. If the meeting began at 9:00 a.m., one needed to be present and ready to get started at 8:45 a.m., no questions asked.

Even the father of our country and first president, George Washington, was known for his dedication to being on time—he would tell Congress he would meet with them at noon and was famous for walking through the doors just as the bell struck twelve. He even applied his habit of being on time to his meals; he always ate at four o'clock. Often times he would invite a member or members of Congress to eat with him. If they were late, they were surprised to find him halfway through or finished with the meal. His comment to the congressman was to the point: "My cook never asks if the company has arrived, but rather has the hour come for the meal to be served?" On one occasion, his secretary was late for a meeting, blaming his watch for his tardiness. Washington's response showed his dislike of tardiness when he told him that he should find a new watch immediately or he (the president) would have to find a new secretary.

Being on time or being late can be a cultural characteristic. Having traveled to thirty different countries in my life to coach individuals and companies, I am amazed that in some countries, tardiness is an accepted way of doing business. On multiple occasions I have traveled to a foreign country to meet with a coaching client only to have them meet me late because the traffic in their city was bad. I flew from halfway around the world and am on time and he is late because of traffic. That is an attitude. He didn't make being on time a priority. If he had, he would have taken into consideration the traffic and left early enough to be early. Now, I am not saying that extraordinary circumstances don't happen that genuinely throw even the best laid plans to be on time off schedule. Things do happen, but they happen far less when being on time is a priority based on one's word and professional image than when it is simply going through the motions and allowing the winds of life to blow one off course. When unforeseen circumstances do occur, I recommend a preemptive approach. Avoid rubbing salt into the wound. Make the first phone call. Never leave your meeting partners sitting around looking at their watches.

Though it is important to be on time when you are invited to meet at a certain time, I believe it is equally important to begin meetings on time. If you have called a meeting or have invited people to attend a presentation, starting on time reflects your degree of professionalism. I can't begin to tell you how many times I have shown up to a meeting early, awaited the start time as announced, only to see the host watch the clock knowing some of the attendees had not yet arrived. The meeting shouldn't begin when all of the attendees arrive; it should start when it was advertised to start. By waiting for others to arrive, you are training them to be late, and you disrespect those who arrived on time.

In business and client relations, it's the little things that can really make a big difference. Winston Churchill said, "Attitude is a little thing that makes a big difference." It is my opinion that being on time is a *big* thing that makes a *huge* difference.

Action Steps:

1. Make a habit of being early so that you are never late.
2. Start meetings at the time advertised, not when the attendees arrive.

Recommended Resources:

Never Be Late Again-7 Cures for the Punctually Challenged, by Diana Delonzor; www.neverbelateagain.com

Attitude Pump 149—No Excuses Here, by John Terhune; www.johnterhune.com/attitude

CHAPTER 12

THE ART OF THE HANDSHAKE

I can feel the twinkle in his eye in his handshake.—Helen Keller

Now you may be thinking to yourself, "What does shaking hands have to do with people skills?" My answer is: a great deal. Think about it. What is the first human exchange when you meet someone, beyond an exchange of pleasantries? In many cultures, it is the handshake. The tradition of the handshake began in the middle ages, when warriors shook hands to signal they were unarmed. Over the centuries, the handshake has evolved into a greeting between strangers, a closing gesture on a business deal, a form of giving one's word, and a confirmation of a bet being made.

There are few things beyond a handshake that will reveal more about you. The quality of the handshake can reveal your levels of self-confidence, compassion, humility, and integrity. The moment of a handshake is when an impression is made. A handshake is more than just a greeting. In business and in life in general, a handshake is an important tool in making the right first impression.

I can safely say I have probably shaken more hands than the average person. Having spoken in front of more than a million people and spent hundreds of hours in reception lines greeting people and taking photos and signing books, I have experienced every kind of handshake known to humankind. Even in countries where the hug and perhaps even the cheek kiss is standard operating procedure for meeting someone, the handshake seems to make its way into part of the greeting process. I have shaken enough hands and experienced enough bad handshakes that I have created my own vernacular to describe the bad ones.

The Vise Grip (someone puts a viselike clamp down on your hand, almost crushing it in the process trying to demonstrate superiority)

The Wet Fish (where someone's hand is wet and clammy)

The Pump Primer (where someone shakes your hand excessively long pumping it all along)

The Politician (where someone shakes your one hand with both of theirs, one of their being on top of yours)

The Three-Finger Gift (where someone offers only a portion of their hand during the handshake)

The Limp Gift (where someone hands you their hand in the form of a noodle to hold instead of grasping your hand with the appropriate pressure)

The "It's Mine, and I Am Not Letting It Go until I Am Ready" (where someone holds your hand, and you can't get it back without a struggle)

The Look Away (where someone is shaking your hand but looking away or down instead of at you)

The "In Your Face" (where someone is shaking your hand and their face is inches from your face; clearly in your personal zone)

The Movie Star (where someone extends their left hand instead of the right hand)

Delivering a proper, polite, and professional handshake is an arrow in your people skills quiver, but it is important not to lose perspective on common sense. There are times when your instincts should dictate your handshake every bit as much as rules. For instance, if you are in another country or doing business within another culture, a good rule is to "do as they do in Rome"; in other words, follow your host's traditions and mirror their handshaking or greeting. A recent example of the "do as they do in Rome" rule happened to me recently when I was on a cruise ship. I was in the gym on the ship and went to introduce myself to one of the instructors. I extended my hand to shake his and in return he extended his fist to bump fists as the more hygene sensitive greeting. Needless to say we exchanged a fist bump rather than a handshake. Assuming normal greeting situations, here are some do's and don'ts to help you make a great first impression.

Use a verbal greeting. Before extending your hand, introduce yourself. "Hi, Bob, my name is John Terhune." Extending your hand should be one part of an introduction, not a replacement for using your voice. By the way, if you can combine that with a nice smile you have scored the greeting trifecta.

One hand is always better than two. Avoid the urge to shake hands with two hands. In fact, a two-handed shake is called the "politician's handshake" because it appears artificially friendly when used on people you barely know. It is always better in business introductions to use only one hand for the shake. The use of two hands, particularly with someone you are meeting for the first time, is simply too personal.

Combine a great handshake with great eye contact. Make sure you are making eye contact with the person with whom you are shaking hands and avoid distractions. I have seen people shaking hands while their eyes never met. Great eye contact while shaking hands with a firm but moderate grip tells the person you are a confident and respectful person.

Moderation is the key. A limp hand is never a good idea when it comes to a business handshake. You should moderate your grip based on the grip you are receiving, but do not get into a power struggle, even if the other person squeezes too hard. Strong and firm can have an aspect of gentle to it if delivered by a humble yet confident person.

A handshake is not a test of strength. A handshake should be a friendly or respectful gesture, not a show of physical strength. An uncomfortable handshake is never a pleasant experience for anyone. Imagine you are opening a door handle and use about the same level of grip in your handshake.

Dry beats wet, every day of the week. If you shake hands with someone who has sweaty palms, do not immediately wipe your hands on your clothing, handkerchief, or tissue. This will further embarrass the person, who is probably already aware of their sweaty hands. You can discreetly wipe them on something and wash them later.

Having shaken many sweaty hands over my career, I learned that there are some people who suffer from hyperhidrosis—wet hands and excessive sweating. If you have this condition, make sure you dry your hands before you shake. Consider having a handkerchief in your hand as you wait.

Know when to end it. A business handshake should be brief and to the point. Holding on for more than three or four seconds can make people feel uncomfortable.

No need to prime the pump. If you shake from the shoulder, using your upper arm instead of just your forearm, you risk jolting your handshake partner. The idea is to connect, not to unhinge.

Shaking hands is a simple act that makes a great first impression. It is always best to follow the social norms of the culture you are visiting. You are being assessed when you touch another hand; doing it properly says a lot about you and how you will be remembered. You are not trying to impress. Your goal is to make the other person feel comfortable.

Action Steps:

1. Ask a successful person in business to assess your handshake.
2. Note the different types of handshakes you receive and think about the impression you were left with.
3. Combine the handshake with a verbal introduction and a smile.

Recommended Resources:

How to Win Friends and Influence People, by Dale Carnegie; www.dalecarnegie. com

Attitude Pump 182—Be in a Constant State of Self-development, by John Terhune; www.johnterhune.com/attitude

CHAPTER 13

THE POWER OF BODY LANGUAGE

Where body language conflicts with the words that are being said, the body language will usually be the more truthful in the sense of revealing true feelings.—Glen Wilson

It would be impossible to come away from trying over two hundred cases and attending more than five thousand live depositions without understanding the power of body language. I began to realize early in my career that body language in most circumstances speaks louder than verbal communication. Your body language is the ultimate truth teller. Your body hears everything your mind says.

Being aware of your body language—of how you physically respond under pressure, what signals you give without intent, how nervousness and stress affects you physically—can help you understand how you are perceived by others. It can also explain how the wrong impression is sometimes given, resulting in confusion. The language conveyed by the physical self should support and enhance what is being communicated verbally. If the visual image differs widely from the spoken message, it is often the nonverbal account that is believed.

If the first step in harnessing the power of body language is recognizing its reality and potential, then the next step is learning how to turn it into a powerful asset. If you were to be a fly on the wall while I conversed with someone, you would see an orchestration of body language that says I am completely engaged in this conversation, I am very interested in what you are saying and you are an important and respected person worthy of attention.

As you may have surmised from my descriptions of witnesses, there is positive body language and there is negative body language. Here are some examples of both.

Positive or welcoming body language:

Maintaining eye contact. There is a substantial difference between just enough and too much eye contact; the last thing anyone wants is to be stared at. When addressing someone, it is important to make eye contact to show you are connecting. When someone won't look at you in the eyes when speaking, he conveys a poor self-image. To be an effective communicator with enhanced people skills, that is the last thing you want to convey. Good eye contact conveys your self-confidence and translates into the other person paying greater attention to what you are saying. Furthermore, it tells the person you are genuinely interested in them.

Smiling. I make a practice of smiling when I meet someone. It sends a message that I am pleased to meet them and that I am a pleasant person worth getting to know. Smiling during conversation can be a signal to the other person that you like what he said, agree with what he said, or are tickled by what he said. It is a gentle but effective aspect of body language that signals you are engaged and enjoying the moment. A smile can be a disarming arrow in your communication quiver, and the more you use it, the more you will be viewed as a person with enhanced people skills.

Sitting squarely on a chair, leaning slightly forward In a one-on-one conversation this is one of my most effective body language tools. By leaning forward during conversation I am saying that I am deeply interested in what is being said by my conversation partner.

Nodding in agreement. Again, this is a body language tool to use sparingly, much as you would an exclamation point. If you are doing it constantly, the gesture loses its effect. Used sparingly, it is a loud signal that you are fully engaged in listening.

A firm handshake. As you have seen this is a subject matter worthy of its own chapter. See chapter 12.

Looking interested. Have you ever spoken to someone and wanted to say. "If you are slightly interested in this conversation would you please tell your body?" Appearing interested can involve a few or all of your available body language signals. The key here is being genuine. Remember, the body hears exactly what the mind is thinking. If you are bored, you are going to convey bored.

Mirroring. Notice how many couples relate to each other. You will see that the partners' postures will match, as if one partner is a mirror reflection of the other. This mirroring indicates interest and approval between people; it serves to reassure others of interest in each other and what they are saying.

Negative or unwelcoming body language:
No eye contact. Very few things drive me crazier than someone speaking to me but not looking at me. I have the urge to grab them by the face and have them look in my eyes. Eye contact shows respect and is a reflection of your self-confidence. Lack of eye contact reveals of your lack of self-confidence.

Crossed arms. Crossing your arms may be natural for you, but it conveys anger or lack of trust to another person. Some experts would call this closed posture. I consciously make sure that I am not in that position when I am talking to someone. When your arms are crossed, you are telling another person that you don't want to be there, you don't like them, and you don't trust them. You may not be thinking that at the moment, but that is what your body language is saying.

Fiddling with hair, fingernails, and so on. I always try to put myself in the shoes of the other person. Would I like it if she were fidgeting with the closest item to keep herself busy so that she didn't have to pay full attention to me? Of course not.

Checking your phone. Turn your phone to vibrate and to remove it from sight so that you are not tempted. I tell people that the only reason I am leaving it on is in case my wife calls with an emergency; other than that, I am all yours.

Yawning. Need I say anything here except to say that this is not positive body language that makes a person feel important? If you do it inadvertently, apologize and explain that you simply had a poor night's rest. If you have been an active listener you will be OK despite your fumble.

Checking your watch. Talk about a signal that you can't wait till this conversation is over. You might as well write him a note telling him he is boring.

Pointing. Pointing your finger at someone is often taken as an act of aggression. If I ever point, it is never *at* the person; that would put them on the defense.

Inattention. This is usually expressed by verbal responses that are not pertinent to what was said.

The key to understanding the role that body language plays in your ability to effectively communicate with your enhanced people skills, is in the realization that your body language is speaking as loud, if not louder, than your spoken word. Being constantly aware of the power of your body language is a vital step in becoming a great listener.

Action Steps:

1. Pay attention to your body language when conversing with others.
2. Pay attention to the body language of those persons with whom you are speaking.
3. Integrate positive body language into your conversations.

Recommended Resources:

The Definitive Book of Body Language, by Alan and Barbara Pease; www. peaseinternational.com

Attitude Pump 123—The Power of Language, by John Terhune; www. johnterhune.com/attitude

CHAPTER 14

BUSINESS MANNERS COUNT

Good manners will open doors that the best education cannot.—Clarence Thomas

Having great business manners will help you stand out from the crowd, and will be one of the most visible ways to display your enhanced people skills. Business experts have been talking about the value of etiquette, including practicing good manners, for close to fifty years. Having good manners will help you any time you make contact with a client or prospective client, regardless of your business, and will tell them who you are as a potential business colleague.

"Manners are a simple exercise in give and take, and they allow our society to function effectively," says Lucinda Holdforth, author of *Why Manners Matter: What Confucius, Jefferson, and Jackie O Knew and You Should Too.* At their most basic, she says, they are "the small kindnesses that make the world a reasonable and decent place."

When I was a kid, my parents were emphatic about my sending thank-you notes for birthday, Christmas, and graduation gifts. As a kid, you understand the importance of doing so; but it is a pain to do it and do it well. As an adult, and particularly an adult in business, simple things like thank-you notes and respectful, timely written communication have come to be the exception rather than the rule.

Recently, I was a presenter at a retreat of CEOs and company presidents in the South Florida area. Before I attended the event, I invested the time to look up the LinkedIn profile and web presence of each attendee. That time resulted in me knowing every person there by name before I arrived. I also knew their job, their alma mater, and a variety of items of interest about them, which made having conversations with each of them easy and natural. For instance, one of the very talented CEOs had a passion as a musician and played with a very successful band. Another CEO had received her undergraduate and graduate degrees from Florida State, my alma mater. It made the conversations flow easily. There were no name badges, and I can't begin to tell you how many people I called by first name said, "You are really good." My response was, "You are my client. I am here to serve. Would you expect anyone in my position to do any less preparation to serve their client?"

Here is where the rubber meets the road when it comes to business manners: I spent the first day home from the retreat composing e-mails to each person with whom I spoke at the retreat. The e-mails were simple, respectful, prompt, brief, and expressed gratitude for the opportunity to meet them and add value to their event and their business. In the e-mail, I offered any assistance that I could render to empower their journey in business and in life. A simple follow-up action that anyone could do, will stand out in the minds of the persons receiving the e-mail. I wasn't asking for anything. The e-mail was about them not about me. Additionally, I took the time to make comments on their blogs or social media pages such as LinkedIn, Facebook, and Twitter.

As time progresses, I will make a point of reconnecting with these people by sending them a quick e-mail when I see articles or blog posts that are relevant to their business. As an example, one of the CEOs owns the most successful staffing business in South Florida. She has won numerous awards for her excellence in the business community. If I see anything related to her industry and her business, which is also her passion, I will forward it to her with a brief note. If I run across someone in South Florida who is looking to hire the right person for an important position within their company, I am going to make that introduction as a means of serving my new friend. People love a relevant introduction, particularly if it can help their business. Good manners show respect for the other person, and you don't use manners as a tool to gain something for yourself. Because all businesses are people businesses first and product businesses second, success in life and business is often about common sense and common courtesy. Unfortunately, common sense and common courtesy are no longer all that common.

Earlier in this book, I referenced the concept of separating your actions from the actions and habits of the other people around you so that you stand out and shine. Really, the concept of separation is about outperforming the average person so that you stand out. The good news is that it is easy to stand out from the average person in today's world; so few people pay attention to the little things that make a big difference. I personally like to create an unfair competitive advantage for myself when I am doing business. That group of CEOs and company presidents I spoke to has invited many speakers over the years, but I would be willing to bet that they received very few notes of appreciation for the invitation and engaging conversation. The expression of gratitude is a great practice in all areas of life, but it will clearly separate you from the masses in business. If you really want to stand out as someone with extraordinary business manners, send a handwritten note on nice stationery. A timely email is nice but it doesn't stand out like a handwritten note.

Action Steps:

1. Reflect on your personal habits specific to your business manners. Could you improve in this area?

2. Rate yourself on a 1–10 scale regarding your effectiveness in demonstrating great manners. One means you are not very good and really need to work to improve. Ten means you are awesome and stand out from the crowd in the way that you demonstrate great business manners. Remember, you always improve what you measure.

3. Determine to separate yourself from the crowd by doing those simple things that will make a difference to other people. Remember, it is about them, not about you.

Recommended Resources:

Business Class: Etiquette Essentials for Success at Work, by Jacqueline Whitmore; www.etiquetteexpert.com

Attitude Pump 154—An Attitude of Delivering Excellence, by John Terhune; www.johnterhune.com/attitude

CHAPTER 15

YOUR ATTITUDE ANNOUNCES YOUR ARRIVAL IN A ROOM

People may hear your words, but they feel your attitude.
—John C. Maxwell

Have you ever seen someone with a great attitude enter the room? She had a bounce to her step, a smile on her face, and an air about her that told the world she is in a happy place in life and comfortable in her own skin. Because of her positive attitude, she was easy to talk with, fun, and engaging. On the other hand, have you ever seen someone enter the room in a terrible mood and a stinky attitude? He was harsh, unfriendly, and unwelcoming in body language and tone. His negative attitude said, "Out of my way or you will get hurt!"

Understand that the attitude you bring to life announces your arrival and sets the tone for your human interactions. A person with a poor attitude simply cannot exhibit the people skills of a person with a great attitude. To a great extent that is because people don't want to be around you, let alone engage with you, when you have a poor attitude. Imagine your attitude as an odor; it either smells great or it stinks. People do not want to be around something that stinks.

For the last two decades, I have been researching and developing content specific to the subject of attitude, and I am convinced that it is your most valuable asset. A person's attitude influences, in a positive or a negative way, every part of her life. It impacts her relationships, energy, stamina, self-image, work habits, willingness to take risks, ability to deal with stressful situations, degree of happiness, and of course, ability to achieve beyond her current circumstances. Your attitude is the most visible manifestation of your people skill set, and acts as a welcome mat or an electric fence—it's your choice.

Give me a person with average talents and a great attitude any day, as opposed to an enormously talented person with a bad attitude. Of all of the physical and mental traits possessed by a human being that will separate one person from the next, attitude stands alone as the great divide between average and peak performance. If you want peak performance from yourself or the people around you, then you must be willing to invest in the development, maintenance, and protection of a world-class attitude. You have to work on it.

Are there times when your attitude is less than exemplary? If the answer is no, then I don't believe you. If the answer is yes, then consider yourself part of the human race. Temporarily losing a great attitude is as human as contracting a cold. It is not a matter of whether it is going to happen; it is a matter of what attitude-recovery system do you have in place to get all the air back in your attitude balloon. In other words, what acts as your emergency rescue system when your attitude is in distress?

Exercise is a predominant attitude-recovery system for many people, including me. Vigorous exercise creates a number of triggers within me that allow me to put things in a proper perspective. The exertion of massive physical effort seems to create a tension release that is always a good first step in adjusting your attitude. Exercise also allows you to connect with a number of foundational principles that create a great attitude in the first place. First, because self-image is such an important building block to a great attitude and to the development of great people skills, anything you do that works on self-image is like hooking up to an oxygen tank when you are starving for air. For me, the exercise of self-discipline fuels my self-image because I know that so few people exercise self-discipline like I do. Exercise depends on one's ability to exercise self-discipline.

I also remind myself through exercise that I am different than most people because I am willing to exercise even when I don't feel like it. Anyone can exercise and push herself when she feels like doing so; but you have to be truly connected to the concept of self-discipline if you are going to exercise when you don't feel like it.

Reconnecting to your dreams, goals, and desires is another effective way of rescuing your attitude. It is important that the activity of each day is anchored to your dreams or goals. If there is no connection, it is natural to feel as though you are simply going through the motions of life and losing the passion that can act as a great foundation for a spectacular attitude. Having a dream that is emotional to your heart will lessen the frequency of losing the quality of your attitude. There are times when pausing with a deep breath and refocusing on your goals is an important mental exercise to reestablish your attitude.

Sometimes it is important to disconnect from the issues causing stress in the first place. There are times in my pursuit of excellence in business that I reach the point of physical and mental exhaustion. At that point, I implement the valuable lesson of walking away for a day or two. Whether it is a walk on the beach with my wife, or a ride on my Harley; sometimes escape from the moment is the best medicine.

As a human being living life, there will be times when your attitude becomes dramatically compromised. When it happens, acknowledge that it is normal, but decide that it will only be temporary, and establish some mechanism in your life to refill your attitude balloon. After all, the quality of your attitude determines the quality of your life. Therefore, work hard to create quality attitude-rescue systems.

I'll bet you've experienced the following scenario. You wake up and feel great; your attitude's phenomenal. Then the drive to work starts. People are beeping and cutting you off. Traffic is slow. Things aren't working right. You get on your mobile phone and try to call somebody, but you get cut off during the middle of the call. You try again, but this time he's busy and can't get back with you. Then by the time you get to work, your parking space is taken by somebody else. The copy machine is jammed, obviously unaware that you must make photocopies for the upcoming meeting. You knock yourself out to get to the meeting on time only to find everyone else is late.

Suddenly your attitude, which started out great, isn't so good anymore. In fact, it's sliding down quickly there are so many things going wrong. The entire day is marked by roadblocks to the expectations you had in mind for this phenomenal day. For many of you, that is almost a daily scenario.

Let me share with you a life lesson and strategy that will make an enormous difference in your life. The difference between average people and people who accomplish extraordinary things, boils down to how those who accomplish the extraordinary maintain and protect a phenomenal outlook during times when the average person starts to lose a grip on his attitude. That is not something that's easy to do. It's something you have to work at, something you have to practice literally on a daily basis.

Any time your attitude starts to slip and things are going wrong, you have to be able to reach down inside of you and hit a default switch that puts you in protection mode: *All right, I am now in a danger zone. A red light is flashing. Sirens are going off. I am now in that zone that is going to make the difference between greatness and average and I've got to reach down inside of me and flip the default switch over to protection mode. I am going to at least maintain the same fantastic attitude that I started with before these circumstances crossed my path. The reason I'm going to do this is that it is my attitude. Nobody else owns my attitude. No other circumstances own my attitude. I own my attitude. There's no one that can take it, steal it, or influence it. It is mine and I refuse to give control of my attitude over to anyone or any circumstances.*

Now here is where being able to recognize where your attitude is, and doing something about it, can separate you from the crowd every day of your life. Discipline yourself: when things are going downhill fast, actually ratchet your attitude up to make your attitude even better. Keep in mind that anybody can have a great attitude when things are going great. Anybody can have a bad attitude when things are going bad. But it takes the true winner to have a really fantastic attitude when things aren't going great.

I cannot tell you how many times defaulting to a better attitude in tough times has created better times. It's amazing how attitude affects results. If you ever get to the point where you can develop that default switch within you, it will put you not only in a maintenance and protection mode, but an enhancement mode when things don't go well. Once this mental muscle gets strong, you are on your way to whatever win you have in mind for your life.

Action Steps:

1. Measure your attitude every day for the next four weeks. Rate your attitude daily on a 1–10 scale. One is terrible; ten is great. Pay attention to the pattern of improved numbers as you are paying attention to your attitude by measuring it daily. We improve what we measure.
2. Determine to improve your attitude over time, recognizing that it is your most important asset.

Recommended Resources:

Attitude Is Everything, by Keith Harrell; www.keithharrell.com

Attitude Pump 151—A Great Attitude Attracts Great People, by John Terhune; www.johnterhune.com/attitude

CHAPTER 16

THE POWER OF YOUR LANGUAGE

Words—so innocent and powerless as they are standing in a dictionary, how potent for good and evil they become in the hands of one who knows how to combine them.—Nathaniel Hawthorne

Language is so incredibly powerful. It actually sends a message to the rest of the world as to who you are. It defines you to others and subtly defines you to yourself. The truth of the matter is that what comes out of your mouth is always the perfect reflection of what is in your heart at that moment. The language you use can either be a warm welcoming sign or a danger sign to other people. This human interaction tool is so powerful that it has the ability to affect the self-image of people with whom you interact. It is so powerful that it has the ability to leave scars that last longer than the cut of a knife. It is so powerful that it can create or destroy lifelong relationships. It is so powerful that it can affect generations of human beings. What a magnificent human interaction tool that God has gifted to us, yet so few of us take the time to understand or even pay the slightest attention to its power and lasting reach. Your style of communication and choice of language impacts other people's opinion of you. Positive communication skills make you seem friendly, smart, and helpful. On the other side of the coin, negative communication skills make you come across as self-centered and superior. People react to us and shape their perceptions of us based on the way we say things to them.

In short, the words and language you use every day have the power of lifting up or tearing down. They have the power of putting someone on the defensive or making someone feel comfortable and welcomed in your presence. Using positive language tends to reduce conflict, improve communication, and reduce defensiveness in others. In the context of your people skill set, you have a choice every day in every conversation to demonstrate your understanding of the power of language by your choice of words. Here are some examples of two different ways to say the same thing; each leaves a totally different impression on the recipient.

- *"Boy, you really blew that one," versus "Let's see what we can learn from this to improve next time."*

- *"I disagree with you," versus "I respectfully disagree with you, but I want to understand your perspective."*

- *"What are you doing?" versus "Would you help me understand your approach to this issue?"*

- *"I need you to do this right now," versus "May I get your help on an urgent task that I need to get done?"*

- *"Good job," versus "I really appreciate your efforts and the pride you take in doing such a good job."*

- *"Are you telling me that you will not have it done on time?" versus "What can I do to help you complete the project on time?"*

- *"Thanks," versus "I really appreciate you."*

- *"What do you think about this?" versus "I value your opinion; what is your perspective?"*

Negative language
- tells the listener what can't be done instead of what can be done;

- includes negative words like don't, not, can't, won't, shouldn't, never;

- assigns blame instead of suggesting a solution; and

- does not focus on positive actions that would be appropriate, or positive consequences.

Positive language
- suggests way to get things done;

- recommends alternatives and choices available to solve the issue;

- has a helpful, personal, and encouraging tone rather than a bureaucratic tone; and

- focuses on positive actions that will result positive outcomes.

I cannot encourage you enough to pay close attention to the language that comes from your mouth. Imagine I could record every word you say tomorrow, without you knowing I was recording you. Imagine further that you and I had the opportunity to listen to that recording at a later date. Would you be proud of the language you used? Would your language reflect a positive attitude and a clear demonstration of great people skills? Would your language tell the world that you are an uplifting person who genuinely cares about other people? Would your language give you away as a person focused on serving instead of being served? Would the recorded language of your day make people want to be friends with you? You have the power to affect people's lives in an incredibly positive way. Are you using this magnificent human interaction tool as a gift or as a weapon?

There are so many people who have accomplished great things in their life whose journey to greatness started with the gift of encouraging words of belief from another human being. Conversely, there have been so many potentially great people who were robbed as a youth of the full extent of their human potential by someone who used language as a weapon instead of a gift.

Remember, your subconscious records everything you say to others and all that you say to yourself. As powerful as the gift of language is as a tool to communicate with others, its power is squared by its effect on you. The subtle voice of your heart is reflected in the way you talk to yourself. Are your inner conversations uplifting? What if I could hear what you say to yourself, your self-talk. Would you be using your inner language as a gift or as a tool for destruction of your self-image? Your self-talk goes a long way toward the development of your personal self-image.

It is a shame that life and your ability to communicate with another human being do not come with a surgeon general's warning. I believe it would read something like this: *Warning, the use of the human empowerment tool called language can be hazardous to the mental and physical health of those persons who come into contact with any person who does not understand the power and lasting effects of their chosen words. It is recommended that you*

112

stay away from persons who demonstrate by their words their lack of training or sensitivity to this incredible human interaction tool.

Recommended Resources:

Words Can Change Your Brain: 12 Conversation Strategies to Build Trust, Resolve Conflict, and Increase Intimacy, by Andrew Newberg and Mark Robert Waldman; www.markrobertwaldman.com

Attitude Pump 123—The Power of Language, by John Terhune; www. johnterhune.com/attitude

CHAPTER 17

DEVELOPING ENHANCED PEOPLE SKILLS IS A DECISION

Commitment is that turning point in your life when you seize the moment and convert it into an opportunity to alter your destiny.—Denis Waitley

In my observation of humans over the last three decades, I can tell you that the biggest hurdle for most people comes in the form of making a quality decision to change and to improve, and then apply a long-term commitment to see the decision through to success. Plenty of people make a decision without it being a quality decision that they follow through on, come hell or high water. For you to develop fabulous people skills that will make all the difference in your personal and professional life, it is going to take a decision to do so, followed by a lifelong commitment to work on you in this area. You really do need to believe that people skills and enhancing them to your greatest potential holds the promise of improvements in every area of your life.

Some of you reading this book already have great people skills, but I believe you can get even better. My challenge to you is to continue to up your game in this critical life skill. Many of you reading this book have average, or perhaps even poor, people skills. Going from great to greater is an admirable goal. Going from average or poor to great is a necessary goal that you should commit to immediately.

Commit to:

➤ Enhancing your attitude.

➤ Enhancing your self-image.

➤ Becoming a keen observer of the people skills (or lack thereof) of other people and learn from those observations.

➤ Smiling more.

➤ Reading more so you can converse with anyone on a wide variety of subjects.

➤ Becoming a great conversationalist.

➤ Becoming a great listener.

➤ Paying attention to body language.

➤ Becoming extremely well read so you can converse intelligently on almost any subject.

➤ Developing a great and polite sense of humor.

➤ Learning to deal with difficult people.

➤ Becoming a person who demonstrates appreciation of others actions.

➤ Becoming a person who is always on time (by always being early).

➤ Becoming a person who is fantastic at remembering people's name.

I am genuine in my belief that you will improve your life, both personally and professionally, by making the enhancement of your people skill set a priority. You will also be setting a fantastic example for family members and work colleagues as you raise the bar in this key skill set area. I highly encourage you to explore the recommended readings listed at the end of each chapter. Remember that success in any area is a process, not an event. Make the enhancement of your people skills a lifelong journey. I am convinced that you will enjoy the journey as well as the results. I look forward to greeting you with a verbal introduction, a firm handshake, and a smile. If we have an appointment you can count on me being early and remembering your name.

Recommended Resources:
Attitude Pump 129—Get Your "But" Out of the Way, by John Terhune; www. johnterhune.com/attitude

PEOPLE SKILLS ASSESSMENT

Check the numbered box that best describes how often the statement applies to you.

5—all of the time.
4—most of the time
3—some of the time
2—rarely
1—never

When complete add up the total points and apply them to the chart after the assessment.

1. I never interrupt to make my point during a conversation.

1	2	3	4	5

2. I always enter into a room with a smile.

1	2	3	4	5

3. I never formulate a response in my head while someone else is talking.

1	2	3	4	5

4. I am always early to appointments and meetings so that I am never late.

1	2	3	4	5

5. I never use curse words in my conversations.

1	2	3	4	5

6. People say I have a great sense of humor.

1	2	3	4	5

7. My body language always conveys that I am fully engaged in a conversation.

1	2	3	4	5

8. I always make great eye contact.

1	2	3	4	5

9. If you asked ten random people in my life, they would tell you I have excellent people skills.

1	2	3	4	5

10. I believe that I have excellent people skills.

1	2	3	4	5

11. I am always in control when dealing with negative or difficult people.

1	2	3	4	5

12. I am excellent at remembering people's names.

1	2	3	4	5

13. I have a defined methodology to remember people's names.

1	2	3	4	5

14. I go out of my way to show my appreciation for people.

1	2	3	4	5

15. I have an excellent self-image.

1	2	3	4	5

16. I always introduce myself verbally, in conjunction with shaking hands with a new acquaintance.

1	2	3	4	5

17. I always have an excellent attitude.

1	2	3	4	5

18. People find it very easy to talk to me about any subject.

1	2	3	4	5

19. I ask great questions during conversations.

1	2	3	4	5

20. People around me often comment on how good I am at remembering people's names.

1	2	3	4	5

21. People would consider me to be a friendly and likeable person.

1	2	3	4	5

22. When I am in a conversation, my conversation partner is doing 70 percent of the talking.

1	2	3	4	5

23. I am an excellent listener.

1	2	3	4	5

24. I am very good at refocusing difficult or negative people away from a problem and toward a solution.

1	2	3	4	5

25. I believe I have an excellent handshake protocol: firm, but not too firm, and I look someone in the eye as I am shaking their hand.

1	2	3	4	5

26. My mind never wanders during a conversation with another person.

1	2	3	4	5

27. I never check my phone when conversing with another person.

1	2	3	4	5

28. People would consider me a very confident yet humble person.

1	2	3	4	5

29. I never try to top the story of another person during conversations.

1	2	3	4	5

30. When I disagree with another person, I do so respectfully and in a manner that invites a respectful back and forth.

1	2	3	4	5

Scoring:
140–150 Excellent People Skills
120–139 Good People Skills
100–119 Average People Skills
Less than 100–Below Average People Skills

ABOUT THE AUTHOR

John Terhune is passionate about empowering individuals and companies to stretch themselves and to understand and then reach their full potential. Believing in his heart that every person and company has the potential to become an unstoppable, goal-accomplishing machine, he combines his expertise, developed over twenty-five years of working with thousands of entrepreneurs around the globe, into a simple "pieces of the puzzle" approach for any individual or company.

With very specific intent, develop a world-class attitude and then combine it with world-class people skills and people centered leadership principles and you will have the all of the pieces in place for extraordinary teamwork and dramatically enhanced and sustainable results.

His riveting and passionate programs have made him one of the world's most in-demand speakers. He has shared the stage with Presidents Ronald Reagan and Gerald Ford; General Norman Schwarzkopf and Lieutenant Colonel Oliver North; football legends Tom Landry and Joe Theismann; and inspirational and motivational figures such as Dr. Norman Vincent Peale, John Maxwell, and Zig Ziglar.

John has authored multiple books on success principles in business and life to include his favorite subjects of entrepreneurship, attitude development, and people skills. One of the most important hats he wears is that of Attitude Coach. In fact, in the last twenty years, he has been an Attitude Coach for over half a million people around the world including entrepreneurs and corporate executives in eighteen different countries.

Currently, John also serves as president of People First International, helping business owners overcome their two greatest obstacles to achieving their goals: low engagement and poor execution. He can show you how to apply the strategic People First Leadership system to close your gaps and eliminate your pain so that you achieve your desired results in these two key areas.

John was raised as the eldest child of a military officer. Moving almost every year until entering college gave John the ability to make friends quickly and to relate to a wide spectrum of people very naturally. To this day, he credits the experience of having to make new friends every year as an important contributing factor to his highly developed people skills. His dream early in life was to become a trial attorney. After graduating with honors from the University of South Florida in Tampa, John was accepted into the prestigious Florida State Law School in Tallahassee.

Upon graduation from FSU Law School, John went on to a career as an assistant state attorney for the State of Florida. During his decade-long career as a prosecutor, he earned top ratings heading up the felony division of his circuit in North Florida, handled over five thousand criminal cases, and won 97 percent of the more than two hundred cases that he tried before juries. While serving as the chief felony prosecutor, John was also an adjunct instructor teaching criminal law, business law, and evidence at multiple colleges.

When not doing business, John Terhune is a passionate husband of more than thirty years, father to three wonderful children, and proud grandfather to two beautiful grandchildren.

To book John Terhune for speaking, workshops or coaching, please contact The Keynote Group at 877.917.7991.

Made in the USA
Charleston, SC
26 March 2015